OUR JOURNEY HOME

OUR JOURNEY HOME

What Parents Are Doing to Preserve Family Values

GARY BAUER

WORD PUBLISHING
Dallas • London • Vancouver • Melbourne

OUR JOURNEY HOME

Library of Congress Cataloging-in-Publication Data:

Bauer, Gary Lee, 1956–
Our journey home : what parents are doing to preserve family values / Gary L. Bauer.
p. cm.
ISBN 0–8499–0931–7 (hc)
0–8499–3568–7 (tp)
1. Family—United States. 2. Social Values. I. Title.
HQ536.B325 1992
306.85'0973—dc20 92–28990
CIP

4 5 9 LB 9 8 7 6 5 4 3 2 1

Printed in the United States of America

This book is dedicated to
my mother, Elizabeth Jane Bauer,
and to all the men and women who
have put family and children first.
Their day-to-day sacrifices have made
possible our long journey home.

Contents

Acknowledgments

A number of people helped make this book possible. First, I want to thank my wife Carol and our children—Elyse, Sarah, and Zachary—for their patience and understanding as I tried, not always successfully, to balance my responsiblity to them with publishing deadlines and my work for the Family Research Council. I'd like to acknowledge the incredible work done by my longtime assistant, Betty Barrett, who transformed my scribblings into actual words on the computer. Finally, I want to thank Charles Donovan and Bill Mattox who provided valuable input and research in their spare time, of which there is little. Last, but by no means least, I want to express my gratitude to Dr. James Dobson whose constant encouragement and advice helped me complete this work.

Gary L. Bauer

1

Going Home

I looked over Jordan, and what did I see,
Coming for to carry me home?
A band of angels coming after me,
Coming for to carry me home.

"Swing Low, Sweet Chariot"

"HONEY, I LOVE YOU. Tell the kids to study hard." In isolation these are certainly not extraordinary words. I have uttered them myself numerous times to end a phone call to my wife while away on a business trip. Millions of other fathers and husbands have routinely said the same. These brief calls, at the end of a day on the road, are one of the family rituals that help knit us together when the demands of work have inevitably separated us. The words used, simple in themselves, are the sound that recall heart and home.

Gulf War Incident

But these words took on special meaning for one family, and I suspect millions of other Americans, when they were spoken in a moment of high stress on nationwide television in the midst of the 1991 Persian Gulf War.

That war offered many images of family, most of them heartrending. We witnessed the tearful partings of husbands from wives; of military mothers from their children, even newborn babies; of grieving parents of killed or wounded soldiers, American, Allied, and Iraqi. History teaches us that war will always bring grief to families (even when justly undertaken to safeguard them), and to this day we have not resolved the unprecedented issues of family separation provoked by the Gulf War.

In the tense early days of that conflict, the Iraqi leadership made a mistake that would be the first of many. After downing some American aircraft, it heartlessly paraded the hapless captured pilots on that country's government-run television network. It was a heavy-handed propaganda ploy designed to lower the morale of American troops and undercut support for the war effort in the United States. The pilots, most looking battered and beaten, were mere "props" in this cynical ploy. Fortunately, the gambit failed and the practice was quickly stopped. But not before some emotional scenes were broadcast into the living rooms of millions of American homes.

My heart broke for these men as my family and I, secure in our own home, watched the drama unfold on the screen. I can only imagine the emotions the pilots' families must have felt seeing their loved ones in such a predicament. But there was one captured pilot, in particular, who left a lasting impression on me. He had been beaten just as the others had, and his face was swollen from injuries suffered in the crash as well as being pummeled by Saddam Hussein's thugs. Fearing for his life, he followed the Iraqi script and unemotionally mumbled, with a leaden voice, a few words of propaganda into the television camera. He was, after all, in the hands of his enemy. But then, unexplainedly, his captors allowed him enough time to speak directly to his loved ones back home in the United States. The POW looked into the camera and, his face softening, said those otherwise mundane words, "Honey, I love you. Tell the kids to study hard."

In four short words a husband assured a waiting wife that, no matter how many miles separated them and no matter what danger may threaten him, his love for her was the first priority in his mind. In six more words the children were reminded that they still had a Dad, that he wanted them to work hard, to achieve the most they could. It was a dramatic display of the love of a father and a testament to the power of heart and home.

Ever since then, whenever I have an opportunity, I have shared this moving episode with audiences across the country. The reaction is always the same. The room usually grows still, tears fall here and there, husbands and wives reach for each other's hands. For most of us the values expressed by that solitary captured POW are the values that motivate and give meaning to our day-to-day lives. These are the reasons we get up in the morning to tackle another day. These are the reasons we work hard, save, sacrifice, and when it doesn't seem possible to go on—we do it all over again. These are the ties that bind.

I have worked in Washington, D.C. for most of my adult life trying to bring some common sense to the laws our government passes. But for most Americans, thankfully, life doesn't revolve around the latest legislation passed by Congress or the most recent double-talk uttered by some high-level bureaucrat. For most of us, even after years of hearing "traditional values" ridiculed, life is still helping hands and good neighbors. It is lovingly packed lunchboxes, nighttime prayers, dinners well talked over, hard work, and a little put away for the future. No government can ever command these things, and no government can ever duplicate them. They are done naturally out of love and a commitment to the future.

That pilot eventually came safely home. I am sure he was sustained in his captivity by faith and the strong family bonds that normally hold us together. I believe millions of other Americans have endured their own form of captivity in recent years. We have been held hostage by a culture that mocks family values. We have seen our most deeply held beliefs ridiculed by sophisticates who disdain these values simply because they are held by common men and women. We have been subjected to assaults on the reliable standards of right and wrong which we try to teach our children. Now, like that POW, we are ready to "go home."

"I'm going home." There may be sweeter phrases in the English language—"I love you," for example. But few phrases pack the emotional wallop as the simple expression of returning to the place of one's birth or to the safe haven of a house well lived in. All of us experience homecomings during our lifetime. Some are grand and nostalgic, as when we return to the streets where we first rode a bike or to the neighborhood where we made the best friends we ever had. Others are bittersweet, because someone we loved is gone or something—maybe everything—is changed. Other homecomings are as routine as pulling into our driveway after a hard day at the factory or at the office.

History and Home

The magnetic draw of hearth and home is richly woven in American history. I remember reading about George Washington's resignation from his post as head of the continental army after the new nation had won its independence. Solemn events were planned around his departure, but Washington was driven by a promise he had made to Martha to eat Christmas dinner with her at his own table, in his own home. He rode hard each day from Philadelphia to Baltimore to Annapolis—the promise driving him to exhaustion. On December 23, his voice breaking, he read his resignation to the Congress and submitted "the interests of our dearest country to the protection of Almighty God . . . to his holy keeping."

Then he was in the saddle riding hard to fulfill the promise—to reach his home at Mount Vernon and there to spend the season of peace on earth. Douglas Southall Freeman, a biographer, described the yearning, the singular purpose that had always driven Washington and which now pushed him home.

> Home was the magnet that drew him, home the haven he sought, home the years-long dream that now was near fulfillment. Every delay was a vexation and every halt a denial. At last the cold, clear waters of the Potomac came in sight, then the ferry and after that the blusterous passage, the last swift stage of the ride, the beloved trees, the yard, the doorway, Martha's embrace and the shrill excited voices of Jack Custis' younger children—all this a richer reward than the addresses of cities, the salute of cannons and the approving words of the President of Congress.[1]

The renowned poet Carl Sandburg wrote about Abraham Lincoln, the fallen president of the restored Union, carried by train from Washington, D.C. back to Illinois. Great crowds gathered throughout Ohio and Indiana to see the train pass by. Bonfires lit the night sky while thousands waved flags and handkerchiefs at the train that carried his coffin and that of his son Willie, too, who would be laid to rest with him. As Lincoln went home one last time, he passed under banners, one reading "To Live in Hearts We Leave Behind Is Not to Die." The train moved through Chicago, the site of the 1860 Republican convention that nominated him, and then on to Joliet where he was met by:

> midnight torches, evergreen arches, twelve thousand people. Every town and village, many a crossroads and lonely farm, spoke its mournful salutation across the house of night and early morning. Here and there an arch or a depot doorway had a short flash "Come Home." At the town of Lincoln was an arch, and a portrait inscribed "With Malice Toward None, with Charity for All."[2]

By the time the coffin reached Springfield, it had traveled seventeen hundred miles and had been seen by more than seven million people. These two men, Washington in triumph, Lincoln in death, went home as men and women always have and always will. They are part of the rich tapestry of a nation always searching for the values of hearth and home.

My Home

There have been many homecomings in my own life. I remember at ten years of age running home, late for dinner after a sandlot ball game that went too long. What a sight that old house was with my father's car parked in front signaling he was home from work. I remember the sound the old iron gate made as I pushed through it. My mouth still waters as I recall the smell of a meat-and-potatoes dinner drifting down through the window. The kind of dinner that (in those days before cholesterol-counting became necessary) was always followed by deep-dish apple pie and a scoop of ice cream.

I remember coming home another day, from high school, when President John F. Kennedy was assassinated. I remember the long walk home and passing the town post office, its flag already at half-staff. Like everyone else I felt a sense of panic and loss unlike anything I had ever experienced. But somehow the sight of that solid red brick house and the knowledge that my mother waited inside were enough to reassure a confused teenaged boy, more than any television commentator could, that we would weather this crisis too.

In a few years there would be weekend trips, my car loaded down with dirty laundry as I sought relief from the rigors of college and weeks of being really away from home for the first time. Today, when I take my family back to the home where I grew up, a million memories flood my mind: The marks on the kitchen door made every couple of months to record how tall I was. My initials carved into the red brick right under the mail box. The stain on the hardwood floor where a chemistry experiment conducted by a budding twelve-year-old scientist went awry. The BB still embedded in my bedroom wall when I learned all guns are loaded. Each room a treasure trove of tales about childhood and growing up to tell my own children.

They love to go to the third floor of the old house so that they can rummage through "the boxes." There in the cartons is the evidence of the life and times of their grandfather, "Pop," as well as of their father. A faded football letter provides an opportunity to tell them about the game where my father scored three touchdowns in shoes two sizes too big (or was it two touchdowns in shoes three sizes too big? Time grows all tales.) A picture of a new graduation class from Marine Corps boot camp is excitedly scanned. There's Pop, shouts Sarah, third row up on the end, taken just days before the men were sent into battle on the murderous islands of the South Pacific. The children sit spellbound listening to the stories of heroism and valor that my father told me late at night, often with tears in his eyes, and that I now pass on to them. How can I possibly make them understand the extraordinary feats done by ordinary men and women to preserve our liberty? These stories are "the mystic chords of memory" that Lincoln said linked patriot graves everywhere.

Sarah excitedly thumbs through a second grade workbook with my name printed in an unsure hand in the front. She counts the number of tests with "100" on them but seems to find more comfort from the occasional "C" or the pages where Mrs. Johnson has written, "Gary needs to work on his addition." Perhaps the papers are reassuring to her. They let her know that you can still make something of yourself even if you are not perfect. I tell them about teachers who made a difference in my life, even when I didn't realize it at the time, about how painfully shy their father once was (and still is), head down in the last row in hopes he wouldn't be called upon. (My first grade teacher wrote to my parents, "Gary must overcome his reluctance to talk." I did, much to the chagrin of my critics.)

Zachary listens wide-eyed as I tell him of schoolyard bullies—of the times I stood my ground and other times I ran away from a guy nicknamed Slugger, hoping somehow in these stories Zachary would learn something that would help him, as a man, come to grips with fear and honor, bravery and courage. They learn, again, that I am not perfect, that their parents' lives and their parents before them had victories and defeats, that we did good and made mistakes, that we sometimes loved and lost and sometimes loved and won. They learn about faith. Each of them begs for and receives one of the childhood Bibles, the pages turning yellow and the covers coming unglued. They love the gold stars pasted in the inside, each one for a verse memorized.

There is a box in the attic back in our home in Virginia, too. As each year passes, it fills with memories and mementos. Someday I suppose my children will take my grandchildren on a treasure hunt through the relics of my life and their childhood. They will find the stacks of letters my parents sent me, letters of love and encouragement through days of doubt in law school, or when I was struggling to find that first job. Maybe they will laugh when they discover their old school papers and wonder at those years when reciting the alphabet and counting to a hundred were the most important things in life. There will be a lot of certificates in the boxes, awards and commissions from my years in government. And pictures, too, at the White House with the President, on Air Force One, or in the Cabinet Room. I guess my grandchildren will be suitably impressed. But when my time has come and gone, I hope my children will tell their own that they remember me most while cheering at a Little League game, playing in the yard, leading a mealtime prayer, or taking a quiet walk. Or perhaps they will recall some bit of wisdom I was able to pass on or the love Carol and I have for each other.

I used to be so impatient with my own parents when they wanted me to just stand still long enough to take a picture of a new suit or when I got into my car, a Ford Falcon Futura, with all my earthly possessions in the back seat, to drive to Washington, D.C. Now I treasure those snapshots that remind me who I was and where I was going and how many mileposts have flashed by.

I came across one the other day of a young boy on a horse. At first I thought it was Zachary, but the print was too old. Then I realized it was too old to be me too—it was my father. But in the photo I can see my blue eyes and Zach's dimpled chin with the face that smiles from top to bottom. All three of us are in that picture—my father, myself, and my son, as well as perhaps the hint of a child yet to be born. And so our lives continue to flow from generation to generation, each of us taking the baton from the one who ran before and passing it to the one who will run next.

Today, I sometimes express frustration that my mother, now a widow, won't sell that old house she has lived in since 1954 and come to live with us. "It's drafty," I tell her. "There's too much crime in the neighborhood. I worry about you." But the truth is, I would miss that old place as much, if not more, than she would. Robert Frost said home is the place where they have to take you in. For most of us, having such a place is vital. We need a sheltered harbor where love is unconditional, where we are recognized and accepted, warts and all—a place where we belong.

It takes a heap o' livin' in a house t'make it
  home,
A heap o' sun an' shadder, an' ye sometimes have
  t' roam
Afore ye really 'preciate the things ye lef' behind,
An' hunger fer 'em somehow, with 'em allus on
  yer mind.

"Home," Edgar A. Guest

Always on Your Mind

Homecomings can be humbling. Many of us leave home convinced we are going to conquer the world. We are anxious to shuck off the restraints of family and traditions, to cut our own swath and make our own rules. At eighteen we know we can do it better, make it faster, and see it all. Somewhere along the way we learn we didn't know quite as much as we thought. Our ideas weren't as new as we took them to be. Suddenly the "quaint," homespun wisdom that was once rejected takes on new life. The first trip home after such an awakening is a return to reality.

I read about a Depression-era man who left New York to find his fortune. Times were hard, and he was soon living the life of a hobo, riding the rails. One day he ran into another vagabond who was returning home and who urged him to do the same. "I can't," the first hobo said. "I left New York to be somebody, and I can't go back until I am."

The two men parted company, but not before the man going home had made the other a present of a pair of good, hole-free shoes, perhaps the greatest sacrifice a poor man on the road can make for another.

This act of generosity overwhelmed the hobo. At first he thought it represented a degree of kindness unlike anything he had ever experienced before. But then he remembered his old neighborhood and the daily acts of caring that routinely took place among his family.

He too returned home, not with the material wealth or reputation he had sought, but with a new pair of shoes on his feet and a sense in his heart that the things that mattered most were not to be found in strange, faraway places. Rather they were right there at home, the place he had fled to search for what he already had.[3]

As I read that story, I couldn't help but wonder if America today isn't a lot like that hobo. Could it be that we need humbly to "go home"? For more than thirty years now we have tossed off many of the rules and restraints painfully learned by trial and error through thousands of years of civilization. Thinking we could have it all and do it all, we went on the equivalent of a national binge. Instead of self-sacrifice, our culture has elevated self-fulfillment as the theme of the hour. Responsibility has been de-emphasized, while at the same time we have created whole new categories of rights—usually rights to unlimited self-expression or some form of self-destructive behavior. Virtue was put on the shelf and blushing (as Mark Twain wrote, humans are the only animals that can blush, or need to) became passé. Faced with an epidemic of venereal disease, our cultural gurus, from Hollywood to the sports arenas, urge us to worship at the altar of "safe sex."

Now we've awakened with a monster hangover. Our schools don't work. Our children are worse off than they were thirty years ago. Over a quarter of them are born out of wedlock. Family breakup is at record levels. Taxes are high, but government wants even more revenue. The federal budget deficit is out of sight, and many state budgets are as bad or worse. The streets aren't safe. In some of our gunfire-wracked cities, even the bassinets aren't safe. We have less time with our families. Even with all the extra hours we spend in the workplace, we are falling behind competitively.

If ever there were a time to go home, this is it.

Some pessimists argue that going home is impossible after this many years on the wrong side of town. We've been away too long, they say. The old house is boarded up, and the folks have moved away and left no forwarding address. The pessimists echo Thomas Wolfe, who wrote, "You can't go home again." Others believe there's no need to call it a night. "The party's still going strong," they say, "things are just fine."

I believe both are wrong. It is possible for us to rediscover our roots and to reclaim the best in our history. After all, this has not been the first generation to have the adjective "lost" applied to it. It is desirable for our people to pull back from disaster and to rededicate ourselves to hearth and home.

In fact, millions of Americans never left home! In spite of all that has happened in the last thirty years, most Americans have resisted the decay in the popular culture. Millions of others are rethinking the lifestyles of the '70s and '80s and finding them unsatisfactory. A counterrevolution is beginning.

Hearth, Home, and Heartland

Signs abound that Americans are indeed "going home." In area after area, from the renewal of religious faith to the rejection of the extreme agenda of a generation of radical feminism, to discontent with the ravages of divorce and promiscuity, the first stirrings of a rebirth of family values are being felt. The signs exist in dozens upon dozens of personal stories, in data tables and graphs, in the dogged refusal of millions of Americans to accept the idea that our nation is too "modern" to care about so backward an institution as the family.

The love of hearth and home knows no social or economic limits in our country. Home is where the heart is whether it's a fashionable suburb or an inner-city flat. In fact it is often in the homes of those with the fewest possessions that the biggest hearts are found. Queen Elizabeth learned this lesson firsthand during her 1991 trip to the United States. Accompanied by Washington, D.C. Mayor Sharon Pratt Kelly and Housing and Urban Development Secretary Jack Kemp, the queen visited the home of sixty-seven-year-old Alice Frazier in one of the toughest drug-ridden neighborhoods in southeast Washington. As the entourage of dignitaries entered her home, Mrs. Frazier, obviously not steeped in the requirements of royal protocol, did what she usually does when a guest crosses her threshold. She rushed forward and hugged a startled and befuddled Queen Elizabeth.

The picture appeared the next day on the front page of the *Washington Post.* I don't know what the reaction of our English cousins was, but the event warmed the hearts of most Americans I talked to. Alice Frazier was obviously proud of her modest home, filled with the aroma of fried chicken and potato salad. It was a public housing unit that she had been able to buy under an innovative program that allows low-income public housing residents to take over their units. It was her home, and as such it was every bit a castle. There are Alice Fraziers all over America—good and decent people who make houses into castles. They are the backbone of the nation, and they deserve better than they get.

A letter to the editor a few days later summed up the emotions many of us felt watching a low-income American welcome royalty to her house.

> In Alice Frazier's house, Queen Elizabeth II was just another human being. She was greeted and treated like any other guest would have been treated. The hug to Alice Frazier was an act of welcome and friendship. She didn't care about the title of her guest or the customs that exist where her guest was from. The Queen was in her house where all are welcomed with a hug.[4]

In spite of thirty years of problems, there is a great reservoir in our country of people who believe in the values of hearth and home. These are the people Governor Bob Casey of Pennsylvania was referring to in his April 1992 speech at Notre Dame. Addressing a group of future lawyers about his state's controversial abortion law then pending before the Supreme Court, Casey reminded the young men and women:

> On either end of our state we have two great urban centers, Philadelphia and Pittsburgh, with all the ferment of big city politics

and big city problems. And in between are millions of people who are right at home in heartland America. Who live in dozens of smaller cities and hundreds of towns—surrounded by the largest rural population you will find anywhere in the country.

And from one end of Pennsylvania to the other, families still raise their kids with the same old-fashioned values that have been handed down from one generation to the next. Values that say, simply, that it's still okay to be a Boy Scout or a Girl Scout. It's okay to say the Pledge of Allegiance at school. To like the *Reader's Digest.*

Where it's still okay to take your family to church, just like your mom and dad took you. Where it's okay to expect your kids to do the same thing with their kids when they grow up.

The governor might just as well have been speaking of the nation as a whole. Between our two great urbanized coastlines, from one end of the United States to the other, families still raise their kids with the same basic values and ideals. Many who live with "big city problems" also struggle to do so. Families still believe, and they're unashamed to say they do.

Research shows Americans are rediscovering the importance of family values. Over 93 percent of us now say that a good family life is "very important." The increase is particularly strong among young people. *U.S. News & World Report* recently found that "two-thirds of . . . voters agree on a set of core conservative values by which to govern society, starting with a belief in the family as the basic social unit, less government, lower taxes and the need for more religion." And *Time* magazine reported that Americans are looking for a standard of living that can't be measured solely in dollars and cents. We are hungry for safe, sane lives, strong families, love, commitment, and values.

In spite of all of our problems, most Americans still believe in the same solid values about which we have always cared. In fact, millions of Americans of all races and economic backgrounds have resisted cultural pressures and have built strong, stable families. Americans are ready for a rebirth of the values and commitments that have served us so well in the past and that hold the only hope for a future that works.

For more than eight years I worked for a president who was known for his unabashed optimism. Ronald Reagan firmly believed, as I do, that America is "a shining city upon a hill," a nation with a special purpose in the unwinding of history. In his first inaugural address, the president outlined his agenda and concluded by saying, "With God's help we can and will resolve the problems which confront us. And after all, why shouldn't we believe that? We are Americans."

I confess to the same optimism. There are reasons for hope. Our problems, while serious, are not as severe as our negative media would lead us to believe. We have economic troubles, but we have lived through depression. We have internal strife, but we have lived through Civil War and global strife. Most of America's families are pulling through. Most households cling together. Most young people aspire to productive, independent lives. Most young adults, upright and responsible, hope to build families of their own. Most families endure.

After thirty years of "experimentation" in which the old values were tossed overboard, there is a great yearning among our people to return "home." We are looking for someone to show us the way. I believe the weakened bonds between husbands and wives and between parents and children can be strengthened again. I believe our neighborhoods can be made safe and our schools can transmit reliable standards of right and wrong. I believe we are capable of teaching our children about virtue, love, and faith. I believe we can come up with a better way to deal with an unwanted pregnancy than abortion. I believe the racial division in our land can be healed and our family life renewed. To paraphrase my one-time boss, why shouldn't we believe these things? We are Americans.

Ask Dad, He Knows

At Christmas, my family, along with millions of other Americans, looks forward to watching the classic Frank Capra film, *It's a Wonderful Life.* And what a classic, heartwarming story it is!

The star is an ordinary small-town figure, George Bailey, played by Jimmy Stewart. The movie chronicles George's life of sacrifice. He gives up a college education so that his brother can go to school. He misses a long-dreamt-of trip to "see the world" to save his deceased father's savings and loan from the evil grasp of Mr. Potter, an American Scrooge. Finally, George settles down and lassos Mary, a girl he's known since high school, but even the wedding is marred. In a turn that is as timely as today's headlines, George is forced to spend all of their honeymoon money to stop a run on the S&L during the dark days of the Depression.

Like most of us, George eventually faces a life-changing crisis. S&L money that mistakenly falls into the hands of Potter, just as the bank auditor arrives, raises the prospect of disaster for George and his family, including financial ruin and possibly time in jail. He has no assets to fall back on—in fact, as the "warped and frustrated" Potter pointedly reminds him, he's worth more dead than alive. In despair, George comes to the brink of suicide, preparing to take the life that had already been sacrificed to the good of so many others. But, on a snow-swept bridge, a bumbling guardian angel named Clarence, trying to earn his wings, intervenes and shows George Bailey what life in Bedford Falls would have been like without him.

It is not a pretty picture. Bedford Falls without George Bailey had become Potterville, a town of gin joints and street brawls where lives were lost, loves unrealized, and tragedies unaverted—all because George Bailey hadn't lived.

The movie ends with a scene that always brings our family to tears. George is brought back to reality—he did exist, his life did make a difference. Then George does the most natural thing in the world for a resurrected man. Rushing pell-mell through the snow-covered streets of Bedford Falls, George finds his way back to hearth and home. There a loving family greets him, and the dozens of people whose lives he has touched gather to bail him out of his crisis. His brother toasts him, "To the richest man in town." George opens a note from Clarence and reads, "Remember no man is a failure who has friends." George and a room teeming with those friends end the movie with a rousing rendition of "Auld Lang Syne." By this point, our family, made up of hopeless romantics, is usually in tears.

I've often wondered what accounts for this film's enduring and remarkable popularity. Jimmy Stewart once suggested that all of Capra's films, and perhaps *It's a Wonderful Life* most of all, are popular because they show "that life's true riches lie in family, country, and God."

I think he is right. And I believe that millions of Americans gather around television sets every year to watch this black-and-white movie because it elevates the ordinary virtues of small-town, middle-class America. Don Feder, a columnist for the *Boston Herald,* explained it this way:

> In an increasingly impersonal, detached world—where people feel isolated, cut off even from their loved ones—this is an urgently needed message: that we count. We may lead what appear to be ordinary, relatively insignificant lives, but in fact shape reality far more than we'll ever know.

Today we yearn for this message. We hunger to know that our lives matter. We want affirmation that home and family are important and that the values of the past are still relevant today. We want to go home. This book is an effort to help you find the way, to give you hope that the permanent things are still alive.

The light that burned in the window of George Bailey's house is lit for us, too. It beckons us to remember what matters and to return to the fold. We should begin that trip now while we still remember the way.

2

Our Dreams

Grandpa tell me 'bout the good old days
Sometimes it feels like this world's gone crazy
Grandpa take me back to yesterday
when the line between right and wrong
didn't seem so hazy
Lovers really fall in love to stay
Stand beside each other come what may
Promise really something people kept
not just something they would say
Families really bowed their heads to pray
Daddies really never go away
Grandpa tell me 'bout the good old days

"Grandpa"

WHERE WILL OUR JOURNEY home take us? What are our dreams and hopes for the future for ourselves and for our children? When we arrive home, how will we know we are there? It's worth taking a moment to reflect on what our country would look like if we were able to recapture the values of hearth and home.

Parents traditionally try to convince their children that they have it "easy" compared to the difficulties the parents themselves faced as children. To the complaint, "I don't like getting up early to catch the school bus," my wife's parents used to respond with the classic, "When we were your age we had to walk five miles to school every day come rain, shine, or snow." When I was growing up, my complaints about low wages from a summer job were countered by my father with long, detailed descriptions of his first backbreaking job at the town steel mill for a pitiful thirty-five cents an hour. Suddenly my job of loading fifty-pound mail sacks on trucks at the Veterans of Foreign Wars headquarters that summer didn't seem as tough. Today my children listen "wide-eyed" when I tell them how I grew up without VCRs, computers, and air conditioning. They wince when I finish with the inevitable, "You don't know how easy you've got it."

These pictures of the past are always a little exaggerated, but they enable one generation to explain to another that things are slowly but surely getting better. But now this tradition may be coming to an end for a simple but shocking reason. New research seems to indicate that for the first time we may be reaching a consensus that life was actually better in the past than it is now. The research is another sign that we are searching for a way to go back to a time of rock-solid values, strong neighborhoods, and intact families.

The study most clearly showing this trend was commissioned in 1992 by the Free Congress Foundation, a conservative think tank in Washington, D.C., headed by activist Paul Weyrich. Their polling firm, Lawrence Research, asked a thousand Americans this central question: "Generally speaking, do you feel that life in America in the past was better than, worse than, or about the same as it is today?" Forty-nine percent of us said we thought American life was better in the past, while only 17 percent thought it was worse.

At first this response seems puzzling. Certainly health and medical care are better now. We have more technological helpmates, from microwaves to VCRs. Transportation is easier and communication faster. Our standard of living is better and our homes are bigger with many more conveniences. What could we be thinking about to cause one-half of us to reject our usual optimism and faith in progress and to see life today as worse than it was in the past?

I believe the study reflects an underlying discontent about matters of the heart and soul. The response to more specific questions support this conclusion: Twenty percent of those surveyed said they believed that family life and home life were better in the past. Twenty percent cited crime and safety—another issue with a direct relationship to the breakdown of the family and the moral relativism of our society. Fourteen percent cited moral values as an area of concern.

Respondents were also specifically asked this question, "Here are some different parts of life in America. For each one I mention, please think of the past and then tell me whether you feel that part of life in the past was better than, worse than, or about the same as it is today?"

"Getting Out of Your Kids' Faces and Into Their Hearts"

a four-part, half-day parenting seminar presented by noted author and speaker

Valerie Bell

9 a.m.-1 p.m. Saturday, May 31
Hosted by

Awana® Clubs International

Complimentary tickets are available at your church, but admission is limited. You must have a ticket to attend, and only the first 500 will be seated. Arrive early to ensure your seat for this excellent opportunity. Additional tickets are available by calling Awana Clubs International.

The seminar will take place at
Awana Clubs International, One East Bode Road, Streamwood, IL 60107
(630) 213-2000

Refreshments will be served.

As an added bonus, the 500 who are seated for the seminar will receive a copy of Valerie's book "How to Get Out of Your Kids' Faces and Into Their Hearts" compliments of Zondervan Publishing House.

Valerie Bell is a writer, speaker, and vocalist who shares her spiritual journey with refreshing honesty. With a warmth and sincerity that's contagious, Valerie challenges her audiences to live out their faith in their everyday world.

Valerie has been featured on the cover of "Today's Christian Woman" magazine, and her many guest appearances on radio and television include "Focus on the Family" with Dr. James Dobson and the *700 Club's* "Heart to Heart" with Sheila Walsh. For more than 10 years (until 1994), Valerie served as a speaker and co-host on the nationally syndicated "Chapel of the Air" radio broadcast with her husband, Steve.

Recently, Valerie has felt God's leading to devote more of her time to writing and speaking. She has written four books -- "Nobody's Children" (Word 1989), which in 1994 was re-released under the title "Reaching Out to Lonely Kids" (Zondervan); "Coming Back: Real-life Stories of Courage from Spiritual Survivors" (Victor Books 1993); **"Getting Out of Your Kids' Faces and Into Their Hearts"** (Zondervan 1995); and her newest book, "She Can Laugh at the Days to Come" (Zondervan 1996). She has also created a new line of audio music cassette tape products including "Prayerwalk ... Care for Body and Soul"; "Prayerwalk II ... Praise, the Practice of Heaven"; and "Classic Prayerwalk ... Blessing Your Community." This unique series of tapes features a creative approach combining aerobic exercise and a focused prayertime to music.

A graduate of Moody Bible Institute and Chicago's American Conservatory of Music, Valerie says she is being "home-schooled" in a hands-on course in parenting by her two sons, Brendan, 21, and Justin, 18. She's married to Rev. Steve Bell, executive director of Concerts of Prayer International.

Valerie Bell

Getting Out of Your Kids' Faces and Into Their Hearts

A Simple Way to Stop Nagging and Start Nurturing

	Better	Worse	Same	No Opinion
Moral values	74	15	10	1
Community and family life	70	15	14	2
Environment	66	21	12	1
Pace of life	64	17	16	3
Economy	62	19	16	2
Quality of workmanship	57	20	20	3
Quality of services	51	26	21	2
Our culture	43	25	27	5

What's more, nearly half of us believe that our grandparents were happier than we are today. Only 29 percent disagreed.

Not only do Americans think that the past was better, they are very specific about the era they find most attractive. Respondents said they thought life before 1910 was worse than today. The same for life in the "Roaring" '20s with its "speakeasies" and gin joints. The decade that most pulls at our heartstrings is the much maligned '50s. Sixty-one percent believe that things were better during those years than they are today. Only 20 percent disagreed.

The '50s? I don't believe it is merely a coincidence that Americans yearn for the decade that our cultural elites constantly mock the most. The '50s was the decade before radical feminism. It was the decade of the baby boom and the growth of suburbia. The most controversial thing happening in the popular culture was the argument about Elvis Presley's swiveling hips. (It certainly seems like a quaint issue now.) Latchkey children, by and large, didn't exist. The school day routinely began with prayer. The illegitimacy rate was a tiny fraction of today's scandalous 27 percent rate. Abortion was permitted in cases of rape and incest but, for the most part, was illegal in the states. No-fault divorce was still just a gleam in some "reformer's" eye. "Gay" meant happy, homosexuality was "in the closet," and placid "Ike" was in the White House. It was the decade of "Ozzie and Harriet" and "Father Knows Best."

Forty years of "progress" later, and we have endured Vietnam, Watergate, political assassinations, the sexual revolution,

AIDS, Madonna, Prince, savings-and-loan scandals, abortion wars, condoms in the schools, pornography, and skyrocketing crime. No wonder many people are tired and desperately seeking a better, more satisfying way to live. Ninety-two percent of us believe we should return to the "manners" of the past, when children were taught to respect their elders and when men gave up their seats and opened doors for women. Eighty-eight percent want to return to the morals of the past, to the time before one-night stands and "condom mania." The same values our elites mock are the values average Americans feel a deep yearning to reestablish in their lives and to pass on to their children.

Even the advertising moguls of Madison Avenue have discovered that we are searching for traditional small-town values. In a sales campaign developed for Kentucky Fried Chicken, the Young and Rubican Advertising Agency created the imaginary town of Lake Edna. Television spots "portray Lake Edna as a commercialized version of Garrison Keillor's Lake Wobegon, crossed with Brigadoon or Utopia."

The results were spectacular. The ads are the most recalled commercial in KFC history. When the campaign began, sales at company-owned stores rose just under 10 percent. More significantly, KFC started getting inquiries that actually assumed Lake Edna really existed. "Would you please tell me where in the world Lake Edna is? It's driving me nuts," wrote one Michigan customer. It is easy to imagine why people might be searching for this make-believe town. We want to find places like Lake Edna, towns where we can live in harmony, avoid crime, and raise our children safe from the influences of a decaying popular culture. While Lake Edna is fictitious, the values it represents are "as much a state of mind as a physical location."[1]

David Blankenhorn, a social policy analyst and president of the Institute for American Values, has conducted an interesting and revealing experiment. He carries a photograph of a traditional, intact family on an outing at the beach in order to get an inkling of the values perspective of the people who are shown it. In it we see a father barbecuing hamburgers and hot dogs while the mother is setting the picnic table. The kids are in the middle of some carefree game, while the family dog plays happily nearby. Blankenhorn has discovered an interesting cultural divide. He reports, "Members of the media and academia elites look at the photo and laugh. They say things like 'That's what I've been fighting against all my life.'" But most people look at it wistfully. One woman said, "I know the 'Ozzie and Harriet' stuff is impossible, but I miss the *familyness* of it."[2]

Of course it is not impossible at all. Millions of families routinely share such happy moments. As I reflect back over the last few years, I don't really think about important meetings I've attended or famous people I've met. Rather it is the family outings at the beach or the park or time together around the backyard grill that most quickly flood my memory. Millions of children are raised in happy homes. Millions of parents stay together through thick and thin. The tragedy is that so many of us feel that this life is no longer realistic or possible.

Status of Women

Many women (and men) feel the pull of hearth and home. Women's rights advocates brag that women today have more opportunities, are more sexually liberated, and have broader horizons. But how do they explain that 55 percent of American women say that the past was better for them (compared to 17 percent who opt for the present)? Apparently millions of women are questioning whether what they have gained in the last thirty-five years is worth what they have lost.

For many women today, it does not seem like progress to know that they are more likely to be abandoned by their husbands, more likely to suffer the trauma of abortion, more likely to be raped or robbed, and more likely to be poor. It doesn't seem very "progressive" when a woman today fears to walk across a dark parking lot or a dimly lit campus. Along with the so-called liberation of recent decades has come a stripping away of the civility that most women desperately want. Sex may be "freer," but the real cost in broken hearts and broken bodies is higher. Love is harder to find and harder to count on.

The sexual revolution has exacted a heavy price—particularly from women. Nearly half of the women entering an abortion clinic have had prior abortions. In most cases they are driven to this traumatic "solution" because the men in their lives have abandoned them and have run from their responsibilities. Rates of pelvic inflammatory disease among women, a leading cause of sterility, have soared in recent years.

As arresting as the numbers are, they give only a hint of the emotional damage. Margaret Liu McConnell, writing in *Commentary*, referred to the impact of the new sexual ethic on women as a "demeaning and rather lonely treadmill" of meaningless sexual encounters, unintended pregnancies, and abortions. "Having premarital sex," one girl wrote, "was the most horrifying experience of my life. It wasn't at all emotionally satisfying or the casually taken experience the world perceives it to be. I felt as if my insides were being exposed and my heart left unattended."[3]

It is true that there are more economic opportunities today, but for millions of women the "opportunities" are really obligations. The average married woman contributes about 30 percent of the family income, not coincidentally, an amount just about equal to the federal and state tax burden on the typical family. One wage earner used to be able to make enough to meet a family's needs. Today millions of women are in the work force because their families can't survive without their income. And in the end they are working to pay Uncle Sam instead of setting money aside for their own families' needs. It is not surprising that many women yearn for a time when they will no longer be as "victimized" as they are in the "enlightened" nineties.

Almost all of these trends are the predictable results of our headlong rush away from hearth and home. In the last year two highly publicized date-rape cases captured the attention of the American public. William Kennedy Smith, a member of the

Kennedy clan, was acquitted, while Mike Tyson, world heavyweight boxing champion, was found guilty. Millions of Americans debated the two controversial verdicts and reached decidedly different conclusions about both episodes. But whatever our perspective, there is a consensus that in the not-so-distant past things were quite different.

In the decade of the '50s all-night bars were not overflowing with young, unattached women on Good Friday, or any Friday night, ready and willing to be picked up by the Willie Smiths of the world. And young women did not go to the hotel rooms of men like Mike Tyson at 2:00 A.M. unless it was for a certain type of illegal business transaction. I am not suggesting that what either woman did somehow excuses sexual assault—it does not. But the "sexual revolution" has changed how some young women weigh these decisions, and it has been a boon for aggressive males who find the universe of exploitable women to be larger now than in the past. The polls consistently show higher support among men than women for the changes in sexual morals of recent years. That's not surprising since men gain the most through the breakdown of the web of tradition and restraint that protected women.

More of us are now asking whether virtue, propriety, discernment, honor, and prudence need to be given a second look. They protected women from aggressive men out to "score," and they provided some sense of ground rules in the eternal dance between men and women.

The Dream for Our Children

My oldest daughter, Elyse, went out on her first real date just as I was working on this book. I had no idea how deep my emotions would run as we approached this milestone in her growing up. Of course, as a father, I was proud that a young man had noticed my daughter and found her interesting and attractive. But what kind of young man is he? Other than that he shared Elyse's involvement in gymnastics, my wife and I knew little about him. What had he been taught at home? At school? What had his eyes and ears soaked in for entertainment? We had a lot of things to talk about before we allowed them to go to a movie.

Of course Elyse was mortified by our questions. She is, after all, a teenager. But I believe she would have been very disappointed if I had not asked those questions. She knows the questions we asked were another reminder that we love her and care about what happens to her. We would never allow a young man to come to our home to borrow our car without finding out a lot about him first. Why in the world would we apply a less stringent set of standards for a boy who wants to "borrow" one of my daughters for the evening?

Elyse and Sarah are precious to me. I don't want either of them to have to worry about date rape. Carol and I are teaching them why virtue is important and why *virgin* is not a bad word. We want them to grow up and live in a country where they can walk down the street and not feel as if they are in danger, where they can go into a convenience store and not find flesh magazines that exploit women and children staring them in the face. I'm hoping that someday they will find husbands who really mean it when they vow to stay with them for richer or poorer, for better or worse. These shouldn't be hopelessly unrealistic dreams. They are the same things you hope for and that all of us want for our children.

Then there is our son Zachary. For too long some families have bought into the philosophy that girls should be virtuous but it is understandable and expected that a young man will "sow his wild oats." This double standard just doesn't hold up under examination. Not surprisingly, at five years of age, Zach's biggest concerns are bumblebees, band-aids, and bicycles. But as he grows up, my wife Carol and I have already decided that we will not fall into the trap of setting one standard for our daughters and another for our son when it comes to the questions of virtue and abstinence. We will teach him, when the time is right, that his manhood is not proven by "conquests" in the backseat of his car, that there is nothing masculine about pressuring a young woman to submit to him, and that women aren't "prey" to be stalked. He will be taught that they, like him, are God's creation to be treated with respect. We will remind him that any girl he is tempted to exploit for his own purposes is somebody's daughter and someday will probably be a wife and mother. Finally, we will tell him that he should not do anything with a young lady that would anger him if he knew another boy was doing the same thing with one of his sisters.

Old fashioned? I suppose it is. But we are desperately in need of some old "fashions." They are absolutely necessary if we are going to rebuild a society based on decency, love, virtue, and faithfulness, and building such a society is not an unrealistic goal. It must be the first order of business on our journey home.

There is, of course, no way to actually go back to the '50s and there are many reasons not to want to, ranging from the segregation of the era to a host of other problems. No time is perfect, but a wise society tries to take the best of each era into the next while discarding what didn't work. That decade's emphasis on hearth and home was important. If we want to enter the next century with a reasonable chance to preserve this great experiment in liberty, we will have to find a way to fulfill the very real yearning we have for a quieter, simpler, saner time.

Rebuilding the Family

What is the rest of our dream? Among other things, going home will mean that there are two parents in each home for more of our children from suburbia to the inner city. This is what society should firmly expect and solidly support. The decline of the two-parent household is strongly linked to a range of problems, from the increasing rate of child poverty to the declines in educational test scores and achievement. Children without a father—or, more rarely, a mother—are missing out on life in a way that transcends politics or class.

As fathers we have a particular responsibility to be there for our children. Father absence is one of the defining characteristics of our age. Tragically, more than a third of our children will go to bed tonight in homes with no father in them. This figure is twice what it was as recently as 1970. A black child born today has only about one chance in twelve of reaching the age of eighteen with his biological father continuously in the home. A white child has better odds, but even then they are only fifty-fifty.

The effect of father absence is profound. Secretary of Health and Human Services Louis Sullivan has pointed out that 70 percent of all juveniles now in our long-term correctional facilities did not live with their fathers when they were growing up. The gangs that plague America's cities are in many ways substitute families for these juveniles, and gang leaders act as substitute fathers. Many of these young people, mostly boys, will have short, violence-filled lives. In the process, they will make our streets unsafe, our families insecure, and our cities increasingly unlivable.

Many experts believe that crime is mostly related to economic conditions. But a 1988 study of more than eleven thousand crimes in Rochester, New York; St. Louis, Missouri; and Tampa-St. Petersburg, Florida found no strong correlation between crime and either poverty or race. The major predictor of violent antisocial behavior was whether or not the individual came from a fatherless home.

Not all, nor even most, children from fatherless homes become criminals or misfits, of course. Millions of women are able to overcome the odds heroically. But most will admit there is little room for error in the process.

Lawrence Mead, associate professor of political science at New York University, has written that "the [economic] inequalities that stem from the work place are now trivial in comparison to those stemming from family structure. What matters for success is less whether your father was rich or poor than whether you knew your father at all."[4]

When daddy left, all too often so did his wallet. Much more importantly, so did the sense of discipline and self-restraint that a father might have imparted. Recovering our sense of the importance of the two-parent family has policy implications, but it is a presumption that must precede policy. Children should be pining at Christmas for two front teeth, not two parents.

A colleague of mine whose daughter attends a large public school in the nation's capital, where an incredible 65 percent of the elementary school-age population comes from a single-parent household, told me how just a short visit to his daughter's classroom would result in a swarm of young boys pulling at his trouser legs and demanding his immediate attention to some project or art work.

"I could hardly fight my way out of the classroom," he told me, "and I felt guilty even trying to leave."

I see this same father hunger in my own children, particularly my son, after even a brief business trip out of town. "Daddy, look what I drew . . . Daddy, I scraped my knee but I didn't cry . . . Daddy, let's wrestle." The words come tumbling out in rapid fire often before my briefcase has touched the floor. Nearly every father has experienced the same welcome.

Many men like my colleague will, in fact, be back in those classrooms as volunteers or mentoring young boys without fathers after school or on weekends. And there's the rub. No one is foolish enough to believe that single parenthood, like poverty, won't always be with us. Moreover, the children of many single parents, through the superhuman efforts of those mothers or fathers trying to bear the responsibility of two people on the shoulders of one, do very well indeed.

But prevalence of a problem—and our attitude toward it—can make all the difference. Programs like the Big Brothers can succeed only if the pool of responsible adult males is large enough to furnish volunteers for each child who needs help. When the pool of responsible adults (or adults with available time) shrinks and the pool of needy children expands as dramatically as they have in many cities, tragedy is unavoidable.

Let me make one final note about the two-parent model. It isn't there as a hammer to pound into the lonely single parent a sense of inferiority about her existence. She knows that loneliness and frustration all too well. For every single mother who spends her days and nights in a crack house, there are a dozen who spend their nights hard at work at a second job to make ends meet. We were vividly reminded of that a few years ago when the Family Research Council cosponsored a focus group in Baltimore with the Institute for American Values in New York.

The focus group is one of those events social scientists and advertisers prize as their invention. It's really just a recreation of the old conversation around gasoline alley or the back fence, primed with a few questions and recorded on tape for analysis. The focus group we cosponsored was asked to talk about issues like family time and to share their fears about raising children in today's world. The participants were drawn from the lower- to upper-middle class, and since we wanted a cross section of the population, several single parents were naturally asked to take part.

Far from trying to defend their lifestyle decisions, the single parents were uniformly outspoken about the difficulty of raising children alone. They spoke movingly about how they wished it could be otherwise. One divorced woman even acknowledged that she was considering reuniting with her husband due to the stress she felt from simultaneously working long hours and striving to be a good parent to her teenage son. She was considering this even though she confessed, "You know, I don't even like him all that much."

Most single parents didn't set out to go through life that way. They want what we all want. I have no idea how one-parent homes are able to juggle responsibilities and keep food on the table. After a taxing week of homework, sleepovers, sports events, and adolescent crises, Carol and I sometimes feel like we need a third adult to help us handle our brood. Raising children is best done as a partnership. Our dream is that more of our children will be raised by both parents while we search for better ways to help those who have only one.

The Measure of Devotion

The two-parent model works best because it maximizes and makes effective the love that nearly all parents feel and struggle to put into practice. It is a love that lays down its life. Sometimes literally.

The Tompkins family—mother and father and their two teenaged sons—lived in a trailer park in Woodbridge, Virginia, a southern suburb of Washington. Last April 9, a fire broke out in the trailer while the family was asleep. Their home was quickly engulfed in flames, but the parents managed to scramble outside. Firemen had already arrived and were trying to rescue the boys, Adam and Benjamin, who were trapped in their room. Neighbors tried to restrain Mrs. Tompkins, but she screamed, "My babies are in there," and rushed into the burning trailer.

One spectator remarked, "She was on fire the moment she went through that door." After the blaze was extinguished, firemen found her body just outside the room where Adam and Benjamin lay dead. This age of ours doesn't value folk wisdom very highly, but it was folk wisdom that one of the Tompkinses' neighbors relied upon when asked to comment by reporters. "I have heard it said," he replied, "that a mother will go through fire for her children, and that's what she did."[5]

It should give us pause to realize that if we were to go by statistics alone, neighborhoods like the Tompkinses' trailer park wouldn't count for much. It would rate low on the income scale and probably very high in dysfunctional families. The experts tell us that abuse and neglect of children are common among the poor. This was probably a neighborhood crawling with social workers checking up on parents. Yet this neighborhood gave us Lillie Tompkins, who shouted "My babies are in there!" and then rushed with them into the arms of a loving God.

Would any of us not do the same? I don't know when I first realized that the lives of my children and of Carol became more important than my own. But I know without a doubt that, like most parents, I would willingly die for my family. Just as importantly, we must live for them.

Right from Wrong

Our journey home will mean that we reestablish reliable standards of right and wrong in our day-to-day lives and in the lives of our children, from our commercial dealings to our relations with friends, neighbors, and family. Americans sense and want this, and they were registering their opinions loud and clear long before their sense of disgust with "things as they are" became a hallmark of the 1992 presidential campaign.

Back in 1989, the Massachusetts Mutual Life Insurance Company commissioned a study of the current state of family values in the United States. They wanted to find out whether family values still existed, precisely what they were, and how important they were to society as a whole. There were some interesting findings on questions related to school prayer, abortion, and other "hot" issues. That those issues remain hotly contested should be of little surprise.

But what was surprising is the fact that large majorities in the poll spoke with great feeling about such issues as permissiveness in raising children and the role of family breakdown in our soaring crime rate and public health problems. They spoke with passion on the importance of having a strict moral code with an emphasis on such specifics as respecting one's parents and authority generally, of believing in God, and being married to the same person for life. All of these were in the top dozen "important values." The '80s have been called the greed decade, but in this study, money-related goals such as "earning a good living" and "having nice things" were well down the list of priorities.[6]

When asked specifically about the causes of crime and other social problems, with a wide variety of replies to choose from, the most frequently cited explanation was hardly what the cultural elite would expect—20 percent of those polled indicated "parents failing to discipline their children." The second most cited cause was similar, "declining family values," picked by 17 percent. In fact, when these factors are added to the fourth and fifth most often cited causes—"the influence of television and movies" and "judges who are too soft and lenient"—some 60 percent of those polled cited issues where traditional values, a clear sense of right and wrong, and the importance of transmitting that sense are directly implicated. Only 10 percent cited some aspect of government programs (either the failures of education or the excesses of social service agencies) as at fault. A lot of Americans apparently believe "our fault lies not in the stars, but in ourselves."

The consistent way adult Americans respond to polls on the general question of values convinces me that restoring reliable standards of right and wrong is not the impossible task that some think it is. When large majorities of our fellow citizens endorse "old-fashioned" virtues and say that morals were better in the 1950s, they must have something similar, something fairly specific in mind. Basic honesty, personal generosity, neighborliness, keeping commitments, being thankful to have a job and getting to it every day on time are all part of it.

When my parents' generation packed their children off to the Saturday afternoon movies (twenty-five cents for a double feature, with previews, cartoons, and maybe a newsreel), they asked, "What's playing?" But for the most part, if it was being shown in the Hippodrome Theater in my hometown of Newport, Kentucky or thousands of other communities on a Saturday afternoon, they didn't have to worry much about what their children might be exposed to. It was wholesome entertainment and it reinforced the right values.

Former Surgeon General C. Everett Koop would have found just the kind of anti-drinking and anti-smoking messages he likes in Walt Disney's *Pinocchio.* The wooden puppet turned real, live boy (was any child ever so clearly the handiwork of a parent's love?) listens to, and promptly ignores, the sweetly crooned advice of Jiminy Cricket to "always let his conscience be his guide." Trouble swiftly follows, and the wayward boy soon finds himself sampling the forbidden delights (all painted in some of the most lurid colors from Disney's extraordinary palette) of Pleasure Island, where thrill-seeking boys are turned into donkeys. Evil is portrayed starkly, not as a liberator but as a baleful puppeteer who will destroy a child's freedom and control his destiny.

A generation later some thoughtful Hollywood moguls decided to update the fairy tale and came out with *Pinocchio and the Emperor of the Night.* In the "new" *Pinocchio,* as in the new morality, evil exists, but its boundaries and significance are blurred. After the new Pinocchio's encounter with Pleasure Island, the film closes with the fairy princess' sweetly burbled admonition to the young boy to guard jealously his "freedom of choice."

I believe "old-fashioned values" and the old Pinocchio are one and the same. Smoking, drinking, and a lot worse happen in both the old and the new world, but, I suspect, they happened a bit less in the old. And when they did, no one insisted that merely different "belief systems" were at work.

As this book was going to press, the Walt Disney Studio was bringing out the original 1940 *Pinocchio* again. I predict the original, with its clear lessons of right and wrong, will thrill children once again and satisfy more than a few parents.

Americans used to have a clear sense of what was right and what was wrong. These reliable standards permeated the whole society and were taught to children at home, church, and in the schools. From our earliest days books like McGuffey's readers and simple, homespun tales, such as the story of George Washington and the cherry tree, were passed on to children to instill simple values like honesty, truthfulness, and integrity. Today we teach about ethics instead of teaching the ethics themselves, we teach children decision making without suggesting what the decisions are that we hope and want them to make. As Allan Bloom wrote in *The Closing of the American Mind,* we reject absolutes except for the absolute belief that everything is relative. And after all that, when some savings and loan executives ripoff their depositors and the taxpayers, when our children cheat on exams, when contractors overcharge on government projects, and politicians are caught with their hands in the cookie jar, we feign surprise.

In the Great Depression people were desperate and hungry. Stealing and law breaking to put food on the table would not have been unexpected. But during those years of want, people routinely slept with their doors unlocked without fear. The crime rate was minuscule compared to today. Now we have more possessions than our grandparents could ever dream of, but in our big cities we sleep behind locked doors and bar-covered windows. It is not material poverty that drives people to violence, it is a poverty of values and a disregard for the value of human life.

Ethics begin at home, too. Regulations and full disclosure laws won't give back to us what we've lost in the permissiveness and lack of self-discipline in private life. What should we expect of leaders in government on issues of greed and manipulation when the rallying cry for so many citizens on social issues, at least since the era of Woodstock, has been "doing your own thing," "self-actualization," or refusing to "impose your values"?

On public radio I recently heard a report from an astonished businessman who had just returned from Japan and thought he saw fairly clearly why that country was pulling ahead of us competitively. He had been in Osaka, a large Japanese city, and had come across an open-air market that was left completely unattended for more than fifteen minutes. During that time hundreds of shoppers milled around, but not one item was stolen. There was a time when the same thing would have routinely happened in America. And it still does in some small communities. But today, can anyone imagine leaving anything of value unguarded for even a moment in New York, Los Angeles, or even in the nation's capital and returning to find it untouched?

Motivational speaker and bestseller author Zig Ziglar makes the same observation: "In Japan, starting in kindergarten, one hour a day, every day, until they graduate from high school, they have a course that teaches students the importance of honesty, positive mental attitude, motivation, responsibility, free enterprise, thrift, respect for authority, patriotism, basic values. That's the reason they are eating our lunch in the market place."[7]

What is the bottom line? Schools need to do a better job teaching values, and churches have a role, too. But the Mass Mutual respondents were nearly unanimous (95 percent) in agreeing that the home is the place where the most basic values are either instilled or not. Knowing that should arm everyone, government officials included, with a new sense of where to locate the ethics-building activities of the future. Full disclosure and term limitations will remain viable policy weapons, but a society that wants a strong ethical foundation in its leaders will find new ways to shore up Mom and Dad's clear yes and no.

Sunshine and Shame

Walter Stewart is a scientist at the National Institutes of Health, part of the U.S. Department of Health and Human Services. He was at one time a benchtop scientist and, by all accounts, quite a good one. But today he has a different job. As chief of the scientific integrity office at our national health centers, it is his responsibility to ferret out and investigate scientific fraud.

That is a large territory to roam, although the vast majority of scientists are reputable men and women dedicated to the highest standards of their profession. But there are exceptions, and those exceptions are the keen interest of Walter Stewart. A short while back, Stewart was invited to address a monthly luncheon sponsored by the largest law firm in Washington, D.C. He was invited to discuss his most famous case to date, a grueling, several-year battle, complete with congressional intervention, over the fabrication of experiments performed under the direction of a Nobel-prize-winning scientist.

Stewart is a direct and unassuming figure, the right qualities to possess when you are speaking to a group of high-powered, buttoned-down lawyers sitting in a posh hotel dining room. He wore a corduroy jacket and no tie, looking for all the world like he had just rushed in from a hectic laboratory or crosstown subway ride. When he finished his remarks, which focused on the way members of professional groups "circle the wagons" when fraud or malpractice is alleged (and often even when it is proved) against one of them, he resumed his seat to warm applause. A colleague of mine leaned over and asked him, "How do you overcome the resistance and get penalties to work to prevent fraud?"

His reply was instantaneous. "No laws or penalties will ever be effective if there isn't shame and the fear of shame. Haven't you found it the same with children? Does any threat of punishment work if there is no shame?" When Zachary comes to me with his head down, his lower lip quivering (it breaks my heart), his voice breaking, to confess some "terrible" deed ("I took a cookie without asking"), it is shame that is at work. Manis Friedman has written a neglected little book entitled, *Doesn't Anyone Blush Anymore?* It is a good question in our jaded age. Unfortunately, among our jaded elites all too often the answer is no. Zachary could teach them something about life!

A Simpler Time

Mike Royko, the flamboyant, plain-talking columnist for the *Chicago Tribune,* relays a story about a simpler time in our country when issues were seen more clearly. The story takes place in the '50s and revolves around a Chicago neighborhood where there lived a self-employed photographer. This fellow, no tower of virtue, made a few bucks on the side by selling nude photos of his poor wife. How she felt about this isn't clear, but a clearer case of exploitation is hard to imagine. He would market them to men at the local bars and factories, and they in turn would sell them to other men. He was always careful not to push the photos in his own neighborhood for fear that his neighbors would discover his sick way of fattening his wallet.

But eventually the photographer made a major mistake. He asked a teenage girl in the next block whether she would pose for him in the same type of photos. The horrified girl promptly told her parents, and our local "porn king" found himself getting a late-night visit from the girl's father and her muscular brother. The two were quickly able to make it clear to the photographer that his health would be in serious jeopardy if he ever came near the girl again.

As luck would have it, a few weeks later the hapless photographer was taking pictures at the local grammar school graduation. The father was also there attending another one of his children's graduation. When he spotted the man, the irate father yelled, "What's that creep doing here? He ain't taking my kid's picture." He then landed a solid punch on the photographer's jaw and explained to the parents and teachers that the fleeing man was a pervert. The photographer moved out of the neighborhood shortly after that. The "heat" and moral indictment of his neighbors was too much to endure. He had to move on.

I love this story. It reflects the power of community censure. It illustrates the authority of a father who stands up for his family. It recalls a time when we knew what a pervert was and a time when we were willing to call such behavior exactly what it is.

Think of the contrast with today's complicated world. Porn is big business and is no longer marketed only in back alleys and bars. In fact what can now be routinely bought at the local convenience store would make the explicit photos of the photographer's wife look pretty tame.

The purveyors of sleaze don't slink out of town in the face of community anger. They build multimillion dollar empires, appear on trendy television shows, and have whole stables of thoroughbred attorneys who defend them and claim that their work is exactly what our Founding Fathers intended when they pledged to one another their "sacred honor." Our Chicago pervert who was exploiting his poor wife could, and surely would, claim today that his photos were really high "art." With a little help he could even apply for a federal grant to pay for the film. Members of Congress would rush to his defense. A guest appearance on Phil Donahue and Oprah Winfrey would swiftly follow. There would surely be a trendy art gallery somewhere that would be willing to display the photos. The outraged father who took matters into his own hands would be the one in trouble—probably jailed for assault and battery—at the very least the target of a civil suit by the pornographer who had been denied his rights of "free expression." The neighbors who made life miserable for the photographer would find themselves labeled censors and religious fanatics. In fact today they would probably hesitate to "impose their values" on the neighborhood porn king. The press would remind us that we are, after all, a pluralistic society. Maybe the wife didn't mind her husband's hobby. Commentators would point out that no one was forced to buy the pictures. If you're offended, just ignore them.

When all the sophistry and verbal gymnastics are over, however, it seems clear to me that that Chicago neighborhood and its residents were a lot healthier in their attitudes than we are today. They knew when to be disgusted. They knew who deserved to be part of the community and who didn't. They knew what to do about it.

Somehow we need to get back to a time when shame helped regulate our appetites. A healthy sense of shame will do plenty to foster recovery from a misdeed, but its major usefulness is as preventive medicine. Our children need now more than ever, when misdeeds with fatal consequences are as close at hand as a turn of a car key in the ignition or a single sexual act, to have that protective shield of shame around them. In a world where an act of adultery with a public official can mean a book contract, or a convicted killer can profit from a made-for-television movie, a world where shamelessness isn't uniformly unrewarding, a profound sense of right and wrong is an even more invaluable commodity.

The *Wall Street Journal,* which usually limits its editorials to such subjects as market deregulation and economic issues, took time out recently to urge its readers to ponder an even more out of date concept—sin. Writing in the wake of stories about Magic Johnson and AIDS, as well as the highly publicized date-rape cases, the *Journal* stated:

> Sin isn't something many people spent much time worrying about in the past 25 years. But we will say this for sin: it at least offered a frame of reference for behavior. When the frame was dismantled during the sexual revolution, we lost the guidewire of personal responsibility, the rules for proper conduct of sexual relations. Everyone was left on his or her own. It now appears many people could have used a road map. They needed to be told the direction their sex life was taking was simply wrong. . . .
>
> This is not an appeal for prudery, but for prudence. The United States has problems with drugs, high school sex, AIDS and rape. None of these will go away until people in positions of responsibility come forward and explain, in frankly moral terms, that some of the things people do nowadays are wrong.

Common Sense

Going home will mean that common sense is put back in the center of American life. There was a time when Americans were known for our homespun wisdom, and the fact is that, even now, the majority of us still bring it to our day-to-day affairs. But, unfortunately, it is a rare commodity in some elite circles. At times we have allowed well-meaning experts to lead us down a dozen blind alleys. And to add insult to injury, another gaggle of experts is usually called in to clean up the mess the first cadre of "intellectuals" created.

American education has suffered most from this foolishness. In the '60s and '70s a lot of common sense was thrown out the window. Remember the open classrooms concept? Some expert decided that children felt unduly constrained by the presence of walls between classrooms. In many places around the country, school boards voted to knock down the walls and teachers began the interesting job of trying to keep twenty-five third graders under control when they could see and hear the twenty-five third graders in the classroom next door.

It was a dumb idea, but only one of many. The same philosophy led some schools to stop giving grades for fear that low marks would hurt youthful psyches. Reliable standards of right and wrong were dropped in favor of teaching kids how to clarify their values. Homework was eliminated because it was "oppressive," an unfair demand on a child's personal time. Discipline rules were relaxed, and elaborate, "due process" systems were put in place before a student could be disciplined or expelled. If you stopped the hypothetical average American on the street and asked him what these changes would produce, he would instinctively know. Classrooms would be unruly, student performance would drop, discipline problems would increase, and education would suffer. And that's exactly what happened. Only the "experts" were surprised by the outcome.

When Bill Bennett was secretary of education and I was under secretary, we authorized a study of the impact of homework. The researchers from Ivy League schools found that kids who were assigned homework and given regular tests did better academically. What a surprise! A quizzical taxpayer once asked Bennett why we had to spend scarce tax research money to discover something that every American parent knew instinctively. It was a good question, and Bennett had a good answer. He reminded the critic that we had abandoned so much common sense in the '60s and '70s that it was now necessary to rediscover the obvious. The experts wouldn't believe mere parents and teachers who knew that homework was important. But if they saw an actual study that reached the same conclusion, it would have credibility.

Every year Washington spends millions of dollars on research products like this one. But there are no secrets to effectively educating children nor to what works. We did so with a high degree of success for several hundred years. It has only been in the last thirty years when we turned the system over to what has been called "educationists," instead of mere teachers, that our problems began to multiply.

Unfortunately, experts still control the educational system at the same time that Americans are hungry for a return to the old-fashioned schools of the past.

Every area of American life has been impacted by this flight from common sense. We turned over our criminal justice system to criminologists, and now the average citizen can't walk without fear on our city streets at night and home security system sales have skyrocketed. Common sense tells us that if we have lax bail and parole laws, we will have more crimes by repeat offenders. Common sense tells us that if you hamstring the police with red tape and second-guess their decisions, you will have emboldened criminals and hesitant sheriffs.

Reclaiming a Sense of Neighborhood

I grew up in a blue-collar neighborhood. The people didn't have many material possessions, but there was a sense of community and belonging. I not only had a mother at home, I had dozens of substitute mothers up and down the length of the street! It didn't do me or my friends any good to be out of sight of the watchful eyes of our own parents. If we violated the rules, I knew my mother would find out about it before I came home to face the music. There was a whole community of "Moms" who kept us on the straight and narrow.

Today, too many of our neighborhoods are empty of responsible adults during the work day. Children are often left to their own devices. We can hardly be surprised if they push the limits of behavior.

On the street where I grew up, heartbreak and joy were shared. When one of us succeeded, we all succeeded. When one of us failed, we were all hurt. I was the first kid on the block to go on to college, and that resulted in a sense of pride, not only in my own house, but among the friends and neighbors who were partners in my upbringing.

When something needed fixing it was often a community project. My father was a maintenance man, but he was unskilled. If there was an electrical problem, Ernie the fireman from across the alley came on over to help out. It wasn't unusual for the men of the neighborhood to join in on a project (putting in a new sidewalk or painting a house, for example) without being asked. The presence of a stranger on the street was quickly noticed and monitored until his intentions were clear.

Today many of us live next to neighbors we never talk to behind closed doors that are always locked. In all the years I played on my street, often into the night, I never felt fear or danger from an adult. Today, in the best of neighborhoods, many of us wisely wouldn't think of letting our children on the streets at night alone. An epidemic of random violence, gangs, drugs, and sexual assaults makes inner-city neighborhoods into streets of fear. Increasingly the suburbs are drawn into the ever-growing circles of violence. No neighborhood seems completely secure. Part of our journey home will involve rediscovering the sense of community and making those values possible for more families and neighborhoods.

Rediscovering Personal Responsibility

Honor used to be an important thing in American life. We took responsibility for our actions. People took pride in their work. When you bought something at the local store, and it didn't work as advertised, you didn't get an argument when you brought it back—you got a refund or a replacement. People have always made mistakes but not too long ago we took responsibility for them. Out-of-wedlock pregnancies didn't just begin in the last twenty-five years, but such an event used to be routinely followed by a marriage. Today a vast bureaucracy at the state and federal level is needed to enforce child support from wayward fathers and millions of women, particularly in our inner cities, are left alone to raise the children.

Relearning Thrift

A penny saved is a penny earned. Old Ben Franklin knew what he was talking about, and through the years millions of Americans followed his homespun common sense. Debt was anathema to my grandparents, and even my parents moved slowly before taking on a long-term liability. People saved before they bought and delayed gratification until later. If they didn't have enough money to buy something with cash, they convinced themselves they didn't need it.

It's hard to know when and how it all changed. But certainly one milestone along the way was the night Frank McNamara ran short of money to pay his dinner bill at a New York restaurant. His wife bailed him out that night, but McNamara who was a partner in a credit firm, came up with the idea of charging people a fee to join a club that would permit them to charge their purchases if they didn't have the cash. Thus Diners Club was born on February 28, 1950. A little more than forty years later 100 million of us carry 750 million credit cards around (7½ cards per person, which is probably the easiest math you will ever hear on this subject). Many of us, following the lead of our government, buy whatever we need whenever we want it. The notion of delayed gratification seems hopelessly out of date. The result is a mountain of debt—personal, corporate, and governmental.

Goals That Won't Be Met, Ends That Won't Meet

For some families there has been virtually no option other than more debt. Families with children are under severe economic pressure today. Decades of neglect—and a handful of conscious decisions—by policymakers have conspired to push families to the perpetual brink of disaster. The politicians and economic trend-watchers are quick to point their fingers at families for overconsumption and a low savings rate. But it is time we recognize that, after paying record-high proportions of their income for such items as housing and health care, many families have very few crumbs left in the cupboard. They cannot save what they do not have.

The federal tax increase on families with children has been particularly severe. In 1948, a typical family of four with two children paid 2 percent of its income in federal taxes. Forty years later they paid 24 percent of their income to Uncle Sam. Income growth has also been sluggish at best. For some groups, it has been a downward spiral. Men between the ages of twenty and twenty-four, a time at which the typical young man is considering marriage, have seen their real annual income decline 25 percent between 1970 and 1987.

Economist Robert Shapiro of the Progressive Policy Institute has pointed out the self-limiting nature of the coping strategies many of today's families have adopted to deal with money pressures. They can be summed up as maternal employment, the birth dearth, and debt.

The family can respond by sending Mom into the labor force. Millions of families have done so, even if on a part-time basis. Between 1960 and 1990, the proportion of mothers in the work force with children under age six rose from 19 percent to 59 percent. If the polls are correct, the majority of these women are not working out of admiration for Murphy Brown. A poll by the firm of Yankelovich, Clancy, and Shulman found that the percentage of women who would "consider giving up work indefinitely" if they "no longer needed the money" shot up 18 points, to 57 percent, between 1989 and 1990.

Once the family has sent two wage earners out into the world, it can go no further—unless we come up with some major backtracking on our child labor laws. The only other alternative is for Mom and Dad to work even longer hours, at the cost of family time, or seek a higher-paying job, a factor not always subject to their desire or control.

The family can also respond by having fewer children, either over the short term to facilitate maternal employment or over the long term to reduce living costs. The evidence suggests that this is indeed happening. Two decades ago, the U.S.

birthrate slipped below the replacement level, where, despite a modest baby boom in recent years, it has remained ever since. Moreover, given the out-of-wedlock baby boom, the U.S. married population is having children at a rate barely two-thirds of replacement level.

Finally, the family can respond by taking on debt. But this too is self-limiting. Eventually the family will reach the ceiling on its line of credit, or interest costs will become too heavy a burden to carry. The family will not seek to borrow more, or the lender will refuse to lend more. In the real world, all of these factors—fewer children, longer hours, credit—will work in tandem as families struggle to get by.

Many families, of course, are defying these trends. As one mother remarked about her decision to stay at home and have a third child, "We'd worry later about how to pay for three college educations. Maybe there would be a discount for that third set of braces or piano lessons."

Responsibility in Washington

We have now reached the point where our national debt is so high it is hard to make the numbers real for average working men and women. On a given day, between sunrise and sunset, our national debt increases by $1 billion. It does that day in and day out, seven days a week, fifty-two weeks a year. In 1992 it took the tax revenues from everyone living west of the Mississippi River just to pay the interest on the national debt. This crushing burden will be passed on to our children and to theirs unless some kind of financial day of reckoning takes place or we find the will and wisdom to get our financial house in order.

This book is about hearth and home. I don't intend to spend a lot of time reviewing the federal budget for you. Suffice it to say there is waste and fraud that could be cleared up to save billions of dollars. There are also programs that it makes no sense to continue funding in the midst of a budget crisis. A billion dollars for three years for public television is a good example. I love many shows on public television, but at a time when children aren't being immunized and our streets are filled with the homeless, doesn't anyone see the logic in reallocating those funds? Public television viewers, if they like the programming, can keep it by increasing their donations.

Not long ago I brought a group of concerned businessmen and women into Washington to meet with some top members of Congress, the administration, and the media. At one session they heard a presentation by Senator Phil Gramm of Texas, one of the rising stars in the United States Congress. Senator Gramm was asked how in the world a member of Congress could decide whether one program or another deserved to be funded given the size of the government and the many conflicting demands on our resources.

Gramm's answer was instructive. He told the crowd that he applied the Dicky Blank test. Dicky Blank, he explained, was a constituent of his in Waco, Texas. Blank ran a printing shop—a family business that he had carefully built up over the years. His wife worked at the shop, as did his older children and other relatives. As the business grew it provided more jobs for people in the community.

Blank worked hard, sometimes sixteen hours a day to make his business go. So immersed was he in his job that when you ran into him at a church social or a Little League game, it wasn't unusual to see ink stains on his hands since he normally had just come from finishing a job. The Dicky Blanks of the world and the families that stand behind them are what keep our country going. Small businesses have been the main generator of new jobs since 1980.

So, Senator Gramm said, "When I see a federal program I ask a simple question. Is the benefit delivered by this program so good, so effective, so beneficial that it justifies taking some of Dicky Blank's hard-earned tax money? If it is, I'll vote to spend it, but if the answer is no, we ought to have the courage to shut the program down and send the bureaucrats who run it back home."

We have come a long way from Ben Franklin's admonishment that a penny saved is a penny earned. But if America is going to go home, one place it will have to begin is with fiscal responsibility, from the kitchen table to the corporate boardroom to the cabinet room.

Remembering Who We Are

The faded black-and-white photo I found in an old shoebox clearly spoke of another time. A dozen faces stared back at me from the picture of a holiday picnic, somewhere around Cincinnati many years ago. From the clothes worn by the people in the photo and the condition of the print, I suspect it was probably taken in the 1920s. The people in it represent the ethnic diversity of the area where I grew up. There were Italians who lived in the area of town affectionately called Spaghetti Hill, Greeks who would start some of the best chili parlors for which the Cincinnati area is still known, and of course, the Germans who settled so heavily in that city and dozens of other places in the Midwest.

There is a lot of talk about diversity in America today, but our country has long had to blend different traditions together in our much acclaimed melting pot. It was never easy, and there was a lot of bigotry to overcome along the way, but somehow we managed to do it.

The men in the photo worked together at places like the breweries in Newport, Kentucky and the Inland Steel Mill in the west end of town or in the dozens of machine tool factories that thrived in the Midwest.

These men and their families built a great nation and saw us through two world wars. And they seemed to do it with less strife and more sense of purpose than we have today.

Why? I think the answer may be in that same old photo. Those dozen Americans are holding a large American flag. It looks a little worse for wear, but it is a powerful image nonetheless. Most of these people were born under different flags; their parents sang other anthems. But now they were Americans. This was home.

Somehow we have to rediscover that unity of purpose. Today we seem to be Americans only because of our address. Everyone wants to put a hyphen in front of their nationality. In our schools we can't even reach a consensus that every child must be taught English. The more that "sensitivity" and "political correctness" are forced on us, the more we appear to grow further apart. The more conscious we become of race, the further we seem to retreat from a color-blind society.

Going home will mean we remember again the power of the words "I am an American." It will mean we start remembering what unites us instead of what drives us apart.

To Dream the Impossible Dream

The rush to reestablish some norms in our daily lives is picking up momentum. In late 1991, a group of thirty scholars from diverse political backgrounds issued a broad platform calling for a society in which "parents put children first, schools do not shirk teaching values, politicians do not cave in to special interests, citizens honor their civic duties and communities take appropriate steps to curb disease and crime." The report went on to contend that the best place to start in building such a community is the family, "where each new generation acquires its moral anchoring."[8]

More astonishing than the statement was the list of those who signed on. They ranged from Richard John Neuhaus, the president of the Religion and Public Life Institute, to Albert Shanker, president of the American Federation of Teachers. The signatories have deep political disagreements among themselves on a host of issues. I have found some of them to be wonderful allies; others have opposed many of my efforts in Washington. It is nothing short of miraculous that this group could put their differences aside long enough to come to an agreement on the basics. But they did, and that is a hopeful sign as America tries to relearn the obvious.

So this is our dream. We want strong families that work, two parents for each child, and stable, safe neighborhoods. We want to reconstruct the web of restraints and respect that once protected women. We want reliable standards of right and wrong to be reemphasized in our schools, homes, and churches. We want to have a moral compass that feels a sense of shame whenever we have failed to defend the weak, protect life, or meet our responsibilities as parents, children, employees, and employers. We want to recover our sense of confidence in each other and in our leaders. We want to regain a sense of thrift in our private lives and fiscal responsibility in our national life. We want to ease the heavy tax burden on families. All of these things are part of the journey home, and that journey can and should begin with our own children right on the streets where we live.

3

The Good News

Three years have gone by. Yes, the sun's come up over a thousand times.

Summers and winters have cracked the mountains a little bit more, and the rains have brought down some of the dirt.

Some babies that weren't even born before have begun talking regular sentences already; and a number of people who thought they were right young and spry have noticed that they can't bound up a flight of stairs like they used to without their heart fluttering a little.

All that can happen in a thousand days.

"Our Town,"
by Thornton Wilder

I STILL VIVIDLY REMEMBER, even though it was more than forty years ago, coming down for breakfast one morning and being surprised to find my father standing alone in the kitchen. He put his arm around me and explained that my grandmother had died during the night. My mother had left early that morning to join her brothers and sisters in making arrangements for the funeral and burial. I was crushed by the news. I had promised Grannie many times that when I grew up I would study to become a doctor so that I could make her aches and pains go away. The actuarial tables don't mean very much to a six-year-old. Suddenly she was gone, and for the first time I had to confront the reality of death.

The Permanent Things

Not long ago, on a cold windy day, I stood at the top of a small hill and looked down at the freshly dug grave of my father. He had suffered a massive heart attack and was now laid to rest. For years he had suffered from severe cardiovascular disease that eventually resulted in the amputation of one leg. I watched him decline from the tough ex-Marine with a swagger, whom everyone referred to as Spike, to an old man who had to depend on others for the basic day-to-day necessities. Now he is gone.

I remember one of the photos of him taken while he was in the service. He looked tan and athletic after weeks of tough Marine Corps basic training. I wonder what thoughts went through his mind as he stared into the lens, his wife on the other side of the country and the future holding the promise of bloody combat in the jungles of the South Pacific. What were his hopes, his dreams? What fears lurked in his heart?

Many years later, after the war was over, he would sometimes give in to my persistent questioning and tell me stories of combat—horrible tales of death, of inhumanity, and of destruction. He had endured things too gruesome for words. He suffered for years from what we now know was combat stress. When July 4 approached each year, the noise of the exploding fireworks would cause him to jump uncontrollably. Each bang was a terrible reminder to him of those fearful hours he had spent crouching in a foxhole while enemy shells exploded overhead.

I know it sounds strange, but now that he is gone, I find myself still unconsciously looking for him. I will wake up in the middle of the night, my mind still fogged with sleep, and for a few seconds I am upset with myself because I haven't talked to him recently. Then suddenly it comes flooding back to my mind that he is gone and words between us are no longer possible.

I wonder if he knew? In spite of the tensions that existed between us, because of his alcoholism and my own stubbornness, was it clear to him that I loved him?

I have so many memories of baseball games, fishing, and wrestling on the living room floor. Now I love doing those things with my children. I remember once "winning" a wrestling match with my father. Now as my son Zachary pushes my arms down and I feign defeat, I wonder what the special magic is that allows five-year-olds to really believe they can beat their fathers!

I take comfort knowing, and I believe it without a doubt, that he is with God. I believe he is whole again, his amputated leg restored, his face smooth, unwrinkled by age, his mind clear again, unfogged by age, his body finally free of the pain. And while we cannot talk face to face, I do still see him in the roundness of my own face, in Zachary's swagger, in the great swirling mix of genes and memory as parent becomes child and child becomes parent.

My blessed mother, herself recovering from her own heart attack, still seems young and vigorous to me. But of course the inevitable cycle of life will claim her too.

It seems that it was just yesterday when the most important thing in my life was opening a ten-cent pack of bubble gum to look for the Frank Robinson All Star baseball card. Then my biggest fears were avoiding the neighborhood bully and getting through Mrs. Johnson's music class without being asked to sing. Now I look in the mirror and see a husband and father staring back, a man worried about mortgages and bills, drugs and the future. My children will someday have Carol and me only in their memories, and then they too will be buffeted by time and their children will mark their passing. It has always been so, it will always be so, until the end of history when the veil of tears will be pierced and our separation from God ended.

The old practice of burying loved ones in cemeteries next to churches demonstrated a great deal of wisdom. Each Sunday, it reminded churchgoers that this life is ephemeral, that it slips through our fingers like sand. No matter how tight a fist we make we cannot stop it from slipping away.

I once read a man's description of a simple walk in the woods in which he "saw both life and death—in the green leaves and the brown, in the standing trees and the fallen. If you are honest when you ask the question, what dies? You must answer, 'Everything the eye sees.'"[1] But the unseen things that only our hearts can understand, go on.

It is obvious that the most important things on this journey cannot be counted and cataloged or assigned a price. No bank balance can give life meaning, and no executive suite or upscale car can be its greatest reward. Rather, it is in what we give to each other and to our children that these brief lives can be measured as a success or failure. It is our faith, our trust, our hope, our kindness, our sacrifice, and our love that ultimately measure who we are. The good news is that in recent years Americans have begun to relearn this central fact. After decades of living for the moment, we are beginning to rededicate ourselves to family and faith.

Just the Facts

A few years ago social analyst and commentator Ben Wattenberg wrote a book that I don't believe received enough attention. It was titled *The Good News Is the Bad News Is Wrong.* Wattenberg argued that in spite of the headlines to the contrary, America was really in much better shape than most people believed. I believe that Wattenberg, in his enthusiasm, overstated his optimistic case. But in many ways he was very close to an important truth.

No one denies that we must confront some difficult challenges. A lot has gone wrong in recent years. A tremendous amount of work will have to be done if we are to rebuild our homes and neighborhoods, stabilize our families and get economic growth going again. But lost in all of the negative statistics and headlines of despair are the hopes, solid values, faith, and the love for hearth and home that have always motivated our people and formed the foundation for the nation. These great national resources can, and must, be replenished in each generation.

Bill Bennett has often observed that we are a traditional people. Put some Americans on an uninhabited planet, and we will do what the early colonists did. First, we will build some houses for the safety of our families and try hard to turn them into homes. We will build a church to give thanks for our blessings and ask for the Lord's protection. Finally, we will build a school, hoping that somehow we can give our children a better shot at life than we had by helping them to know more. We are traditional, and we are looking for ways to put those values back to work.

One of my great frustrations during the time I served in government was the inclination of bureaucrats and social scientists to spend all their time dwelling on what was not working. All the attention and resources are focused on the dysfunctional family, the failed school, and the declining neighborhood. Wouldn't it be better for us to examine what works, and to build on those strengths to solve the pressing problems we know we must confront?

As it turns out, there is a lot of good news. Away from the unreality of Washington, D.C., and the fake glitz of Madison Avenue and Hollywood, the same rock-solid values prevail in the heartland of America.

Political analyst and commentator Fred Barnes has observed that,

> Families who hold to traditional values get scant media attention, and the little they get is often scornful. Still, their values thrive—not in trendy restaurants and boutiques, but all over America in homes with children. The old virtues are quietly exalted in suburbs and rural areas and urban residential neighborhoods where families live.

Everywhere, even in the wreckage of our modern culture, there are signs of life that seem to point to an overwhelming desire to return to basic values. The Massachusetts Mutual Life Insurance Company study I mentioned earlier discovered that Americans were placing increasing importance on family values and were turning away from materialism as a guiding principle in their lives.

Those of us who said that having nice things was a very important value declined by 10 percentage points, from 36 percent to 26 percent. These percentage shifts don't just represent an attempt by those asked to impress the pollsters. Charitable groups are reporting an upsurge in our willingness to help those less fortunate. In 1989 alone, charitable giving was up 10 percent to a record $114.7 billion. We are putting our bodies on the line, too. Ninety-eight million Americans, half of all adults, did volunteer work for charitable organizations in 1989—up 23 percent in two years.[2]

There has also been a significant increase in the percentage of Americans who said that respecting one's parents and respecting one's children are their most important values. And in a dramatic shift of attitudes since 1989, 84 percent of adults strongly agreed that "family is the place where most basic values are instilled"—a rise of 22 percentage points.

Perhaps the best news of all is that we are rediscovering the joys of family life and of children. For most of this century the trend lines have been against the values of hearth and home. More mothers entered the work force, more infants were placed in child care, more boys and girls became latchkey children, more marriages failed, and more couples chose careers over nurturing. Often these decisions had good reasons. Many couples couldn't pay for their basic necessities without two incomes, a new emphasis on equality opened opportunities in the work force for women who weren't there before, and some marriages ended because the women in them would no longer tolerate physical abuse. No one is in a position to second-guess these decisions, but a price has been paid in the overall health of our children.

"From the child's point of view, the break-up of the family has been very unambiguously unhappy," says Karl Zinsmeister of the American Enterprise Institute. "The data are monolithically worrisome. None of these circumstances—divorce, single-parent families, step-parent families—are healthy. There is no precedent for what has happened in any other time, in any other place."[3] Now, increasingly, Americans are looking for ways to return to a strong family life and put children first.

Mom Rediscovered

A few years ago at a conference on children, best-selling author Sylvia Hewlett shared a story about her successful effort to convince a national accounting firm—Arthur Anderson—to begin a day-care program at work. The day-care center was necessary because many of the women at the company put in sixty-hour weeks after the birth of their children.

This solution was no doubt good for Arthur Anderson. But the story prompted one analyst to ask, "What kind of human society urgently encourages its new parents to hold sixty-hour-a-week jobs as if nothing changed when their child was born? . . .

Is tax preparation and figure juggling (or any other paid occupation) really so urgent and noble an undertaking as to justify sacrificing the welfare of our children?"[4]

There are now signs that a growing number of women are deciding that children come first. In fact, a new consensus is emerging on the importance of maternal care in the raising of children.

- A 1989 *Washington Post*/ABC News poll found that eight out of ten parents with children under age fourteen believe it is best for children to be cared for by a mother at home.
- A 1989 University of Michigan study found that most employed mothers opting for care by family members do so out of preference rather than necessity.
- A 1989 *USA Today* survey found that 73 percent of all two-parent families would have Mom stay home full time with the children if money were not an issue.

This parental preference for care by family members is widely shared by the public at large. For example:

- A 1989 Lou Harris poll found that 82 percent of the American public believes care by parents or other family members is superior to care by nonrelatives.
- A 1989 poll commissioned by the Massachusetts Mutual Life Insurance Company found that Americans believe parents having less time to spend with their families is the single most important reason for the decline of family values in our society.
- A 1989 Gallup poll found that by a five-to-two margin, Americans believe it is better for families to make economic sacrifices so that children can be cared for by a mother at home than to maximize family income to improve their economic standing.

- A 1990 *Times-Mirror* poll found that 73 percent of all Americans believe that too many children are being raised in day care, up from 68 percent in 1987.

Back to the Home

The increase in the proportion of Americans concerned about children in day care is only one indication that the work-and-family pendulum is beginning to swing back toward home. According to surveys taken by the Yankelovich, Clancy, and Shulman polling firm, the proportion of all employed women who would consider giving up work indefinitely if they no longer needed the money shot up eighteen percentage points (from 39 to 57 percent) between 1989 and 1990. Similarly, the proportion of adults who believe a child is likely to suffer if the mother works outside the home rose from 48 to 55 percent between 1989 and 1990, according to the *Washington Post.* And the proportion of teens who told the American Chicle Youth Poll that they want their mothers to stay home jumped from 34 percent in 1986 to 48 percent in 1990.

Most surprising of all, 23 percent of employed baby boom women, the major recipients of the new equality of opportunity in the work force, say they plan to quit work *altogether* within five years. If it happens, this would be an extraordinary shift in attitude.[5]

Even professional feminists are conceding that the pendulum is swinging. Feminist philosopher Betty Friedan now admits, "In the first stage of modern feminism there was a defensiveness which was probably necessary against defining women only in terms of their child care and family roles." But now, "It's time to change the rhetoric and admit that many women want nothing more than to stay home with their children."[6]

Nearly 30 percent of working women polled last year in the Yankelovich survey responded that "wanting to put more energy into being a good homemaker and mother" was a good enough reason to consider giving up work entirely. This is the highest figure in more than twenty years and an 11 percent increase over 1989.

My colleague, William R. Mattox, Jr., director of policy analysis at the Family Research Council, has reviewed all of the research and polls and reached a startling conclusion: "During the past two to three years, there has been nothing short of a dramatic change in the way in which women and men view questions of work and family. The pendulum appears, at least at an attitudinal level, to be swinging back in the direction of home. Men and women, in large numbers, are expressing concern about not having enough time for their children."[7]

It is unlikely that many women in the '90s will abandon the work force permanently. Economic pressures alone will probably prevent that. But many women are looking for alternatives.

Working at Home

With the advent of more convenient technology from FAX machines to home computers, an increasing number of mothers are finding ways to work from home. This almost ideal approach can help provide badly needed income while also making it possible to be there when children come home from school.

There are an increasing number of resources for women who want to start home businesses. *Home Work* is a national newsletter for home-based businesses. A sample issue for $3 can be obtained from Home Work Newsletter, P.O. Box 394, Simsbury, Connecticut 06070. Also of interest is *Home Businesses Under $5000,* a thirty-six-page beginner's guide to sixty-five home business ventures. It costs $5 and is available from Sun Features, Box 368, Cardiff, California 92007.

Other women do appear to be taking a new look at "sequencing"—going in and out of the work force to accommodate their family situation at the time. The idea of being a superwoman who can hold down a full-time job, keep a home, nurture children, and then go out for a night on the town with her husband is increasingly seen by many women as an unrealistic lifestyle.

Sequencing is not a new concept. Arlene Rossen Cardoza, the author of a book entitled *Sequencing*, has pointed out some pretty well-known examples of women in public life who took time out from their careers to nurture children, including former British Prime Minister Margaret Thatcher, former United Nations Ambassador Jeane Kirkpatrick, and U.S. Supreme Court Justice Sandra Day O'Connor.

Countless women who are not household names are doing the same thing. As our family grew, Carol shifted from working full time, to working part time, and finally to being a full-time homemaker. I suspect when our children are older Carol will reenter the job market. In the meantime, we are fortunate to be able to get along financially without a second paycheck. Not every family can. Millions of women who don't want to be away from their children have been forced into the workplace—and that is a national tragedy.

Family Time Famine

Changing attitudes are at least partly rooted in a growing perception that parents today do not spend enough time with their children. A 1990 *Los Angeles Times* poll found that 57 percent of all fathers and 55 percent of all mothers feel guilty about spending too little time with their children. A 1989 *New York Times* survey found that 83 percent of employed mothers and 72 percent of employed fathers say they are torn between their job demands and the desire to spend more time with their children. And a 1988 *USA Today* poll found that parents with young children identify "missing big events in their children's lives" as the thing they most dislike about their current day-care situation.

The perception that families spend too little time together is based on reality. A recent Family Research Council study found that parental time with children has declined roughly 40 percent since 1965. Americans also increasingly sense that unfriendly cultural changes have made unhurried parental time with children even more important today than it was a generation ago. Whereas June and Ward Cleaver's biggest worry was that their sons might get caught up in some of Eddie Haskell's schoolboy pranks, today's parents have to contend with much weightier fears: drugs and guns in schools, sex abuse in day care, teen pregnancy, AIDS, and youth suicide.

In confronting such problems, however, parents today have fewer allies. A generation ago, parents looked to the schools, youth organizations, and even the media to reinforce the values they wanted transmitted to their children. Far from being allies, these social institutions today are often viewed by parents as part of the problem rather than part of the solution. Thirty minutes of the Fox Network's "Married . . . with Children" and a trip to the school-based condom dispensary help to explain why.

It is too early to tell just how much the growing concern about America's family time famine is affecting parental behavior. There is some recent evidence that the decades-long rise in maternal employment has stalled and may even be receding a bit. During the twelve-month period preceding June 1991, the percentage of employed women between the ages of twenty and forty-four fell for the first time since the Labor Department began keeping such figures in 1948. During this twelve-month period, the number of nonemployed women in this age bracket increased nearly 320,000. Labor officials attributed more than nine-tenths of this increase to a rise in the number of women "keeping house."

These trends may continue. A lot of young people have grown up without much parental attention. They are now part of the twenty-something generation that is entering young adulthood and preparing for careers and families of their own. There are some indications that this generation intends to commit more time to family and children than their parents did.

They're not thinking just about so-called quality time either. Chicago's Leo Burnett ad agency has studied the mood and tastes of the twenty-something generation. It discovered "a surprising amount of anger and resentment about their absentee parents." Burnett's research director said, "The flashback was instantaneous and so hot you could feel it."[8] Nearly 65 percent of this generation is saying that they will spend more time with their children than their parents spent with them. "My generation will be the family generation," says Mara Brock of Kansas City. "I don't want my kids to go through what my parents put me through."

Here Comes Dad

It is not just mothers who are rediscovering the job of raising children to responsible adulthood. Many fathers, too, are beginning to reevaluate their priorities. As James Levine, director of the Fatherhood Project, a nonprofit clearinghouse, says, "Fathers are beginning to talk about the same issues that working mothers are struggling with. They are trying to figure out ways to cut down from their 12 hour work days. They're leaving the office early enough to eat dinner with their kids and then they're working at home for a few hours."[9]

Robert Half International, the world's largest financial accounting, data processing, and financial recruiters, conducted a nationwide survey of men and women that seems to support the same conclusion. Max Messmer, chairman of Robert Half, said that the survey showed that "both men and women are saying that they're willing to accept reduced income and slower career growth in order to be more involved with their families."[10]

The *Wall Street Journal* has highlighted this trend, although it has focused on highly paid executives who have more leeway to rearrange their priorities than do many working-class families. One executive who took a 50 percent cut in pay so he could spend more time with his family was quoted as saying, "I used to be on the train to work before they were even awake, but now I can get them off to school. And I have memories I never would have had—like seeing my daughter's face light up when I meet her at the school bus. That's become more important to me than power and prestige."[11]

Hollywood and Home

Even in jaded Hollywood, the land of quick divorce and avant-garde lifestyles, there seems to be the stirrings of a renewal of hearth and home. Sigourney Weaver, the star of the *Alien* movies, has publicly talked about how her priorities have changed with marriage and children. Speaking of the challenges in raising her daughter Charlotte, she said, "I've much more patience and energy than I would have predicted as someone who never really was interested in children. It's what do you want at the end of your life? Do you want to have 50 films? . . . Or do you want pictures of your grandchildren? It's great women have to face that dilemma.

"When people talk about the power list, a lot of us (women) who could be on it have better things to do. Which is taking care of our kids and families. And that's a lovely thing to do with your life."[12]

Harrison Ford can boast of starring in three of the five all-time box office hits. He has an eight-hundred-acre spread in Wyoming, a home in Los Angeles, and an apartment in New York. But when asked about his accomplishment and his wealth, he talks instead about his two young children, Malcolm and Georgia. "It seems like all I've been doing for the last 25 years . . . I realize that what's most sustaining is having kids."[13]

Even Jane Fonda, now settling down with media mogul Ted Turner, seems to be reevaluating her priorities. She told an interviewer, "I was driven every moment of my life. What's important to me now are rest and replenishment and feeling safe and secure with somebody. That's what Ted is for me, and the few things I regret in my life are . . . not having put enough time into mothering, wiving, taking care of the inner life."[14]

That doesn't sound much like the Jane Fonda, "Hanoi Jane" as she was derisively called, who sat smiling at a North Vietnamese machine gun battery and acted as if she were shooting down American pilots. But in recent years even the most radical oddballs of the '60s and '70s seem to be reevaluating their flight from country, hearth, and home.

The reordering of priorities can be seen in the movies coming out of Hollywood, too. It is no coincidence that three well-received movies in 1991 had this as a central theme—*City Slickers, Regarding Henry,* and *The Doctor.*

These Hollywood stars are not leading the way, however. They are just reflecting the changes in attitude that are taking place in many communities and neighborhoods. We have seen it among our own circle of friends in the "go-go" world of Washington, D.C. Many mothers are switching to part-time work in order to have more time with their children. Some of my male friends have made conscious decisions to be home earlier and forgo weekends at the office. It is more than being burnt out; it is a renewed awareness of what life's richest rewards are and where they are to be found. Family bonds are never "junk."

This shift didn't occur overnight. *Newsweek* magazine reported several years ago that Americans were ready to choose family over money. The Gallup poll captured the mood when it asked, "Which do you feel is more important for a family these days: to make some financial sacrifices so that one parent can stay home to raise the children or to have both parents working so the family can benefit from the highest possible income?" A parent at home won handily by 68 to 27 percent.

In fact, given a choice of two career paths—one with flexible full-time work hours and more family time on a slower career track—the other with inflexible work hours on a faster career track—78 percent chose the slower, family-oriented career path.

Rabbi Harold Kushner, the author of *When All You've Ever Wanted Isn't Enough* believes the '90s and beyond will witness a sea change in attitudes:

> We are going to see a more idealistic America, where career professionals are going to say, "My integrity is more important than

> my income, my family is more important than my job title, watching my daughter in her ballet performance or watching my son in his Little League game is more important to me than working late at the office."[15]

Kushner contends that for a long time we bought into three myths:

- Doing something that makes money is more valuable than doing something that shapes people's souls.
- Working with numbers is more valuable than working with human beings.
- Dealing with adults is more valuable than dealing with children.

But now we see the myths for what they are. Now home and family beckon.

Not by Bread Alone

I am not suggesting that economic growth is not important. A vibrant economy enables families to care for their children, buy a house, and provide for the future. The steady economic growth of the '80s resulted in more than 18 million new jobs. When that growth stopped in the early '90s, there was real pain and suffering.

But more of us seem to understand that the biggest assets we have cannot be readily tallied in a financial statement. By the same token, the most important resources a nation has cannot be computed in its gross national product. There is nothing wrong with wealth, but things alone are not enough to make life worth living.

It is a poor man who has never fallen in love nor held a crying child, regardless of what his bank statement says. There are many individuals of modest means, even poverty stricken, who are rich with friends.

Instinctively, most of us know these things even though our culture sometimes entices us down a dead-end road in the pursuit of power, fame, and money. For many of us it takes a crisis to get our priorities in line. For some, unfortunately, the truth is discovered too late.

Lee Atwater, in the final months of his life, wrote movingly about life and love. I knew Lee personally. He had a reputation as a tough competitor, and he was. We had our share of disagreements. When you took on Lee, you always knew when it was over that you had been in a fight.

On March 5, 1990, Lee's world abruptly changed. When he got out of bed that morning he was on top of the world. In 1988, at the age of thirty-seven, he had managed George Bush's winning presidential campaign. He was rewarded with the chairmanship of the Republican party—thus realizing one of his lifetime goals. His delightful wife, Sally, was pregnant with their third child. Lee was nailing down plans to cut a rhythm-and-blues album with B. B. King, one of his idols, fulfilling another dream. As Lee put it himself, "I was one cocky guy."

Later that day he was giving a major fund-raising speech in Washington. He was delivering the speech with his usual enthusiasm, when suddenly his left foot started to shake. Lee tried to press ahead with his remarks, but then the whole left side of his body began to move uncontrollably. Eventually he collapsed and was rushed to George Washington University Medical Center. By that evening he had been given the devastating news that he was suffering from a brain tumor and was in a fight for his life.

In the months that followed, Lee fought the killer inside him and he also fought to understand what was really important in life. Suddenly walking in the corridors of power didn't seem so significant. Lee confessed that he "felt guilty about the degree to which my career and my illness had robbed me of critical time with my children." He was able to reconcile with his father, who was also fighting cancer. He came to know God and spent long hours in conversation with friends who could help him develop his faith.

In one of the last articles Lee wrote, he talked about the acquisition of wealth, power, and prestige. Then he confessed, "What power wouldn't I trade for a little more time with my family? What price wouldn't I pay for an evening with friends? It took a deadly illness to put me eye to eye with that truth, but it is a truth the country can learn on my dime."

Not many of us can name the top ten corporate executives in America, or ten leading U.S. senators. Few, except for political junkies, can name the members of the Bush cabinet or the biggest Wall Street high rollers. But all of us can name our best friends and the people who love us. Our own experiences tell us what is really important.

The Family That Eats Together

Even the family meal is making a comeback! A *New York Times*/CBS News poll found that eight out of ten people had eaten dinner with their family the night before. And the experts are now conceding that such time together is of great importance. William Mattox of the Family Research Council has written,

> One of the things that makes the family strong is the tendency to gather together for regular rituals and routine activities that everyone is part of. The meal is the most routine and the most symbolic. It's a rich time for social interaction between family members and a time when emotional needs are nourished.

When I worked at the White House I often infuriated some of my colleagues by my insistence on being home for dinner whenever possible. It was worth the heat I took.

Don't misunderstand me. If dinner at your house is anything like dinner at mine, it is not all sweetness and light. It is around that table that I often hear from Sarah for the first time about a spelling test that didn't quite work out or a long explanation from Zachary about why he wasn't a good boy today. Victories and good news are brought to that table, and so are childhood hearts broken by a first love. In that brief hour together we shed the load of worries we have been carrying all day and help tend to each other's wounds.

Carol always fixes a healthy meal, but the real sustenance received is not on our plates, but in the words that pass between us. There won't be that many more years when the Bauer family will be able to routinely gather around the table together at the end of a long day for a meal "well talked over." Elyse, our oldest, is only a few years away from college. I will miss these simple times when we, as a family, renew our souls as much as our bodies.

Call Me Old Fashioned But . . .

The daily papers are filled with stories about child abuse, drunkenness, violence, and family disintegration, but these are still the exception, not the rule. According to the Times Mirror Center for the People and the Press, 86 percent of us agree with the statement, "I have old-fashioned values about family and marriage." Nearly as many (70 percent) agree that "there are clear guidelines about what's good or evil that apply to everyone regardless of their situation." So much for the situation ethics that are being taught in many of our elementary and secondary schools, as well as on our university campuses. Most of us just don't buy it!

Baby boomers, usually thought of as liberal and hostile to traditional values, now appear to be leading the charge back home. When they were asked whether the country was better off or worse off because of recent changes in our culture, 59 percent of the boomers chose worse off because of more permissive attitudes on sex, 67 percent said worse off because of increased single parenting and 72 percent selected worse off because of less religious training for children.

Being a boomer myself, I am not surprised by these results. In my own circle of friends and acquaintances, I have seen tremendous tragedy, most of it due to the breakdown in values. It is among my generation that illegitimacy has skyrocketed and venereal diseases have gone wild. Many of my peers have relearned the old lessons of life the hard way—by suffering the consequences of breaking those rules.

I believe these hard knocks are reflected in the way many in my generation are now raising their own children. The conventional wisdom thought these liberal younger Americans would reject the so-called old-fashioned approach. But when *Rolling Stone* magazine posed that question, they were surprised to find that nearly half of the baby boomers now embraced the same child-rearing values that their parents emphasized. They wanted their children to experience a strong family bond, religion, duty, responsibility, and accountability. They wanted them to believe in the work ethic and honesty and to have good manners. Another 32 percent were emphasizing discipline and respect for authority as they raised their own children.

When Carol and I were newly married it was easy to be theoretical about how we were going to raise our children before we had any. But there is nothing like a toddler to give you a little perspective on the need for discipline. And there is something about the admiring glance of a fourteen-year-old boy in the direction of your oldest daughter that gives you a whole new outlook and concern about old-fashioned ideas like virtue and chastity.

Parent Gap

In recent years we have heard a lot about the generation gap, the division between young and old, and the gender gap, the differences of opinions between men and women. But increasingly the defining division of our time may be the family gap. Married people with children have decidedly more conservative views on a host of issues than do single adults and even those who are married with no children. The very act of raising a child, of trying to bring another human being who is dependent on you to responsible adulthood, profoundly alters the way we think about the issues and events of our time.

Carol and I have experienced the transformation in our own lives. Getting married changed some of our youthful attitudes. But it wasn't until Elyse came along, and then Sarah and Zachary, that the changes became pronounced. In college it was easy to engage in purely abstract discussions about drug legalization or theories of child raising. But once you hold a newborn in your arms—your child, flesh of your flesh, blood of your blood—theory recedes and the long arduous task of nurturing and protecting begins.

Youthful Wisdom?

The evidence of the growing shift toward hearth and home is also apparent among the young. A generation that has experienced the trauma of divorce, the absence of parents, and a culture heavily laden with sex and violence may now be ready to look for a more traditional approach.

In fact, Irma Zandl, a "trend predictor" who specializes in working with children, believes that is exactly what is happening. Her insights on future trends are avidly sought by corporate giants like General Motors, Johnson & Johnson, Chesebrough-Pond's, and Nabisco. Her work is unearthing a tremendous shift in attitudes among the young.

Zandl reports that many teenage girls are rejecting the role of superwoman trying to balance family and career. Instead they say they want families first with careers to follow later. "It has become a phenomenal trend. They're saying they want to be great wives and mothers. . . . Many of them talk about how they want to stay home until their kids start school, at least," she says.

"They say they want careers where they can work with children. . . . They say they are never going to get divorces. . . . Thirty-four percent of the girls say 'The Brady Bunch' (with its emphasis on family values) is their favorite rerun. 'Murphy Brown' is never mentioned."

Zandl believes these youthful attitudes are a reaction to the trends in the '80s. Many of these young people were latchkey children, and now "they want to come home to a warm house instead of an empty house. . . . They have very positive core values. Family, friends and children are taking a pre-eminent place in their lives." Zandl predicts that these teenagers will start getting married younger and start their families younger—reversing the trends of the last thirty years.[16]

The more conservative trend is apparent in other ways too. A poll released by *USA Today* on sex, morals, and AIDS asked this question: "Does the safe-sex message trouble you because it might condone casual sex?" Fifty-four percent of adults agreed that the safe-sex message was dangerous, but a whopping 63 percent of the teenagers surveyed said they thought it was. When was the last time young people had more conservative attitudes about sex than their elders did? Apparently our children understand the moral implications of this issue even better than some of their parents.

Most young people place a high value on such goals as having children and a happy family life and living closer to parents and other relatives. Significant majorities of adolescents also express agreement with the values of their parents, and generally the number doing so in 1990 is higher than the number in 1975. Over time, young people are likely to reflect the changes taking place in the generation that went through the 1967 Summer of Love and is now enduring the 1992 Winter of Their Discontent and all its second thoughts about the value of the sex-and-drugs revolution.

Aging is itself a conservatizing process, as is marriage, but becoming a parent causes the biggest change of all. (As someone once remarked, "A conservative is a liberal with a teenage daughter.") But the apple, even when young, does not fall far from the tree. In 1990, 71 percent of young people told researchers from the University of Michigan that they agree with their parents about what to do with their lives; 69 percent agreed with Mom and Dad about religion; and 86 percent about the value of education. Admittedly, the numbers for "politics" and "what is permitted" on a date were somewhat less impressive, just under

50 percent. But I predict time will bring those numbers more in line, too.

As young people mature, however, the tendency to return to the nest, emotionally and in every other way, is strong. Just four years after high school, the percentage of young men and women who say that being successful at work and having lots of money are important declines sharply (the latter to under one-third for men and one-fifth for women). The percentages saying it is very important to have a happy family life soar to 87 percent for men and 88 percent for women. No gender gap here! The figures suggest that the vast majority of young people do "go home" in their lifetimes. It's vitally important, of course, that someone be there to greet them when they do.

That Old-Time Religion

At one time or another, roughly two-thirds of the baby boomers dropped out of organized religion, but in recent years more than one-third of the dropouts have returned. More than 80 percent of the boomers consider themselves religious and believe in life after death.

In fact after thirty years of increased secularization of our public life, most Americans have had enough and appear to be yearning for a return to that old-time religion. Overwhelming majorities believe that voluntary Bible classes and prayers should be permitted in public schools, and 55 percent of us believe that religion has too little influence in American life. Sixty-three percent of us are willing to take our views into the ballot box by not voting for a presidential candidate who does not believe in God.

In the intellectual precincts occupied by our cultural elite the influence of religion on public life is still seen as dangerous. The Supreme Court provided the latest evidence of this foolishness on June 25, 1992 when it struck down as unconstitutional nonsectarian prayers at high school graduations. This was only the latest in a long stretch of cases that seek to separate Americans from our most deeply honored traditions. Justice Antonin

Scalia spoke for a minority of the Court but for the majority of the American people when he referred to the Court's reasoning as senseless.

As I listened over dinner with my family to this case being announced on the evening news, I couldn't help but think back to 1962. That was the year of the first Supreme Court decision that struck down prayer to begin the school day. I was a sophomore in high school at the time.

I was so angered by the decision that my classmates and I organized a protest. We plastered signs objecting to the ruling on the walls at Newport High School. We held rallies and led students who agreed with us to local churches for prayer *before* school. More importantly, at the age of sixteen, I decided that I would devote my life to fighting in the public arena for the values of family and faith.

Thirty years have gone by and the Court still has not found its bearings. Few things in life are certain, but this one is: These rulings will be challenged. The traditions of faith, family, and freedom are too deeply interwoven in the fabric of our history for the ruling in this case to endure. Three decades after the Supreme Court's first assault on the religious tradition of communities, the American people still overwhelmingly support the role of religious values and religious observance in public life. The roots of that tradition run too deep, its branches are raised too high, for the Court's mistaken judgment to stand.

On issues of religious liberty, the Supreme Court continues to scrape against the bedrock of the American spirit. It's an awesome conflict to watch, but in the long run I have no doubt that it is the spirit of the people that will prevail.

In 1992 *Newsweek* magazine reported the results of a poll showing that 57 percent of Americans say they pray every day and 78 percent say they do so once a week. Fewer than 10 percent of women and 15 percent of men say they never pray at all. The 1991 Gallup poll from the Princeton Religion Research Center showed similar responses to questions asked of Americans about the importance of religion in their lives. As the year ended, some

58 percent of Americans said that they felt religion was "very important," up from 53 percent in 1987 and the highest annual figure in years.

Some of the most important moments in our home are built around prayer. Our two girls pray on their own now when they turn in for the night. But I usually slip into Zachary's room in the evening to pray with him before bedtime just as my father used to do with me. On the wall of our son's room there hangs a beautiful print of a father praying over his son while an angel bars the window from the evil lurking outside. Not all that long ago I probably would have thought the picture was melodramatic, but now as I tuck in my own flesh and blood and ask God to keep him safe, the evils of the world outside seem very real.

In our universities many young people are taught that when you become "educated" you shed silly, irrational things like faith, religion, and prayer. But in the real world, when life is about begetting and getting through the day, we learn anew that it is faith that gets us to the finish line.

The popular culture still ridicules religion and often treats it like the plague, but that will change too. Even normally secular *Time* magazine believes that the separation of church and state has gone too far. In a special report at the end of 1991, *Time* concluded,

> For God to be kept out of the classroom or out of America's public debate by nervous school administrators or overcautious politicians serves no one's interests. That restriction prevents people from drawing on the country's rich and diverse religious heritage for guidance, and it degrades the nation's moral discourse by placing a whole realm of theological reasoning out of bounds. The price of that sort of quarantine, at a time of moral dislocation, is—and has been—far too high. The courts need to find a better balance between separation and accommodation—and Americans need to respect the new religious freedom they would gain as a result.[17]

That's what the numbers are showing. Poll after poll, study after study, are all pointing to a rediscovery of family values, hard work, religious faith, and a rejection of materialism and hedonism. But polls reflect people's attitudes; they don't always tell us what is actually happening. We may claim to believe one thing while we continue to do another. What about the real world of our day-to-day lives? Are there signs of renewal there? Thankfully the answer is yes.

4

More Good News

Where we love is home,
Home that our feet may leave,
but not our hearts.

"Homesick in Heaven,"
Oliver Wendell Holmes

AMID THE DEPRESSING NEWS that came out of Los Angeles during the Rodney King riots, there was an occasional ray of sunshine. One such story was carried by the Associated Press in the *Washington Times* about a single wedding between two Los Angeles residents:

> The bride's wedding dress was stolen. The groom's tux was looted. And the camera-man and limousine service canceled at the last minute after rioting tore apart south central Los Angeles.
>
> But in the love-conquers-all tradition, Victoria Le Melle and Roger Compton walked down the aisle Saturday in a church fragrant with carnations, white roses and smoke from the fires that nearly ruined their nuptials.
>
> "I am happy anyway," the new Mrs. Compton, a 28-year-old bus driver, said yesterday. "We just decided we weren't going to let a bunch of ignorant people get in our way. May the 2nd was our day, and nobody was going to stop us."[1]

These newlyweds, like countless couples before them, took a leap of faith. Surrounded by looting, arson, death, and destruction, and armed only with their love for each other, the Comptons decided to begin the most exciting adventure of their lives. We should all pray that they succeed and that thousands of other inner-city residents follow their lead. It is couples like these who will ultimately help American cities begin the long journey home.

Back to the Altar

The institution of marriage is much stronger than the popular culture would have us believe. It's true that no-fault divorce has made the institution more vulnerable, but the divorce rate leveled off a decade ago and is now declining. It peaked at 5.3 percent in 1981 and has dropped to 4.7 percent in 1990. And, in fact, most of us do find happiness at home—with our spouses.

It is impossible to put into words what the love Carol and I share with each other means to my life. Ours is not a storybook relationship. From my experience, few good marriages just "happen." They take hard work and effort. There are good days and bad. Like most husbands and wives, we argue at times. We are both constantly exhausted and often too tired to have much time or energy left for each other at the end of a long day. I can assure you that I am far from being a perfect husband.

But in countless ways Carol reminds me of her love, in notes in my lunch bag (yes, I still "bag it," I hate those fancy D.C. restaurants), in her loving care of our children, in the constant effort to keep the house neat, in her words of encouragement when I am down or have just suffered one of the inevitable defeats that Washington regularly serves up.

A year or so ago, Carol planned to take the children to Rochester, New York to visit her sister and her family. A project at work just wouldn't let me get away. I was looking forward, however, to a bachelor weekend. I had big plans—all rather vague—but enticing. Home Alone! I was going to be on my own again.

Finally the time came for them to leave. I kissed Carol and the kids and waved good-bye from the top of the driveway. Then I bounded back into the house to begin my big weekend. Three rented videos and four junk meals later I felt lost, alone, and depressed.

It wasn't just her meals I missed. It was the simple home chatter, the exchange of glances, piling into the car with the kids to go on errands, laughing together, giving Zach his bath and getting one in return, and going to church together. In short, all of the give and take of family life. I was lost without them. When they finally returned home a few days later, it was hard to figure out who was more excited, our dog Jumper or me.

I am not exceptional in this regard. Most of my married friends feel the same way. By and large, I believe our love of married life, its joys and disappointments, is shared by our friends and neighbors. It is what most Americans want or are desperately searching for, someone to spend their lives with.

Parents magazine polled its subscribers and found that 88 percent of us would get married again, 82 percent to the same person, if we had it to do all over again. According to Dr. Marilyn Ruman, a clinical psychologist in California, "Marriage has become 'in' again." Social scientists have pointed to the growing numbers of young Americans who have not married as proof that the institution has lost its appeal, but the same *Parents* magazine poll shows that 70 percent of singles indicate they want to be married. In fact, most of them eventually will be. While marriage is being delayed, the overwhelming majority of men and women are looking for a spouse and hope to bring children into the world. It is a tragedy that many who want to marry can't find an eligible mate, but it is not a sign that marriage has been rejected as an institution.

Promises to Keep

Fidelity is also "in" again. *Self* magazine asked its readers if they would ever consider having an extramarital affair even if no one would find out. Eighty-six percent of women said they would not, and 67 percent of the men agreed. *Self*'s surprised editor-in-chief looked at the results and concluded, "Some recent public statements about the overall disintegration of the moral fiber of the American family may contain a bit of hyperbole." In both surveys the magazine discovered that most marriages "are surprisingly strong." And keep in mind these results were from the readership of a magazine that emphasizes individual needs over commitment to others.

I have never quite understood the position of those who argue that it is of no concern if a political leader is unfaithful. I believe it does matter if a candidate for office, or any of the rest of us, commits adultery.

Adultery is the breaking of a promise. This marriage promise is generally made in the presence of God and witnesses. We vow to remain faithful until death, to forsake all others. And those witnesses are usually the most important people in our lives: fathers and mothers, brothers and sisters, closest of friends, dearest of relations. When we break *that* promise, made before God and those witnesses, it says something important about our regard for promises generally.

Likewise, the inauguration of a president of the United States is a very formal event, not unlike a wedding. All the pomp and ceremony are orchestrated around the taking of an oath and the delivery of an address. The oath and the address consist of words that are recited in the presence of God and thousands of witnesses. George Washington made it a point at the first inauguration to put his hand on the Bible. He added four words to the oath spelled out in the Constitution, on which the ink was barely dry. Washington said: "So help me God."

I believe adultery will always matter, just as all promise breaking matters. As long as we elect presidents, as long as they run on platforms and make speeches, as long as we administer oaths to them, their promises will matter. We all have promises to keep.

Where's Dad?

The country is no longer content to watch family values decline and tragedy increase. Parents from the inner city to the suburbs are looking for leadership that will speak the truth about families, children, and values. I believe we are on the verge of a great national debate about family, faith, and freedom.

The opening rounds of that debate may have started on May 19, 1992 when Vice-President Dan Quayle gave a major speech on the poverty of values at the Commonwealth Club of California in San Francisco. Quayle said,

> Children need love and discipline. They need mothers and fathers. A welfare check is not a husband. The state is not a father. It is from parents that children learn how to behave in society; it is from parents above all that children come to understand values and themselves as men and women, mothers and fathers.

He added,

> It's time to talk about family, hard work, integrity and personal responsibility. We cannot be embarrassed out of our belief that two parents, married to each other, are better in most cases for children than one. That honest work is better than handouts—or crime. That we are our brothers' keepers. That it's worth making an effort, even when the rewards aren't immediate.

Quayle's remarks caused a firestorm, particularly when he suggested that a popular television show, "Murphy Brown," had sent the wrong message when it glamorized the leading character having an out-of-wedlock child. Within hours Quayle was being pummeled by outraged Hollywood columnists and by the national media who accused him of making another "gaffe." The White House, always nervous about controversy, first supported Quayle and then appeared to back off.

Diane English, the producer of "Murphy Brown," fired off a statement suggesting that if Quayle didn't like illegitimacy, he should support abortion on demand. She would be right if those were the only two alternatives we could offer young women, but they aren't. In the days that followed I found myself on the front lines again trying to defend the obvious—that our culture needs more intact families. In fact, the vice-president's office was so overwhelmed with interview requests that his staff couldn't handle them all. I filled in whenever I could. In the two-day firestorm that followed, I debated the issue on scores of television shows including the CBS and NBC

Nightly News and the prestigious "MacNeil-Lehrer Report" and in dozens of newspaper interviews with the *Washington Post, New York Times,* and *USA Today.*

On CBS "Morning News" I debated Ann Lewis, the sister of far-left Congressman Barney Frank, who is also one of only two openly homosexual members of Congress. Before our debate began, a brief report aired revealing that Harry Smith, the soft-spoken co-host of the show, had just been named father of the year. It provided a great opportunity for me to congratulate him and then add, "But Harry, it isn't just your children who need a great father and mother. All of our children need two parents working together to raise kids. If we can't agree on that, the country really is in deep trouble." The debate was smooth sailing from there. Harry Smith's award had made my point—children missed Dads too.

Dear Ms. English

Later that day I sent an open letter to Diane English, the producer of "Murphy Brown." In part it said:

> It is a sad commentary when extremely talented people like yourself and the acting professionals associated with your popular program devote those talents to characterizations that completely misread a crisis afflicting our nation's cities and families.
>
> The American family is in trouble—everywhere. In America's inner cities, the problem is particularly acute, but the trends are accelerating at the greatest rate in less economically distressed areas.
>
> Children are beginning life without fathers. Their mothers are beginning family life without husbands. It is a *situation tragedy.* The numbers are heartbreaking and mind-numbing.
>
> We Americans who proudly hold many records and can boast of many accomplishments are winning the international Olympics in family breakdown, hands-down. We lead the major industrialized countries in category after category when we'd rather not even be in the race: in divorce, in the total number of

single-parent households, and in the percentage of single-parent households as a proportion of all households.

Over 40 percent of all pregnancies conceived in the United States today are out-of-wedlock. Despite 1.6 million abortions a year—for which we would earn another Olympic gold—over a quarter of all children are born out-of-wedlock. In our nation's capital, the numbers approach 65 percent of all births. In some neighborhoods in our cities, it is 80 percent.

"Out-of-wedlock" almost always means "fatherless." But these children have fathers—their mothers did not become pregnant alone. Their loneliness, and their children's, comes later.

Fatherless means there will be no one there to say, "Come on," when the four-year-old boy wants to wrestle with his Dad, or "That's enough," when the fourteen-year-old boy-man wants to fight it out with his buddies on the streets. Fatherlessness means a new generation of young girls growing up looking for an image of manhood, and probably finding it in another boy-man who is all too willing to exploit her desire for closeness and abandon her to begin the cycle anew.

Most single mothers struggle heroically to do their jobs and to raise their children successfully. But the odds are steeper for them, and they will be the first to tell you. They do not make $175,00 a year, or work at glamorous jobs. They can't afford even to visit the hair stylist, much less enjoy the free services of the typical news anchor's make-up artists. Fifty-five percent of them are poor, five times the rate for families with both a mother and father.

This is the hard truth. But perhaps the harder truth is that every time a popular figure, either in real life or in the attenuated life of a television series, lends glitz to a spouse-and-marriage-free existence, the lights in this land that should be a Shining City on a Hill grow ever dimmer.

Vice-President Quayle was right on the money. If we care about this society, we will do all we can to cease depicting violence as pleasurable, out-of-wedlock sex as rewarding and cosmopolitan, and the traditional family as irrelevant and out of fashion.

A few weeks ago the entire nation witnessed the bitter fruits of the extinction of hope when virtue collapses, family fails, and hatred rises. You could see the fires burning on any

> television screen in America. You could see it from the Hollywood Hills.
>
> It is time we all took these issues seriously, examine seriously why this nation's families fell off the tracks twenty-five years ago, and recognize why the vice-president's message is the best news our nation's homes and neighborhoods have heard in a long, long time.

I wasn't the only one who agreed with the vice-president. Dr. Sonya Friedman, the host of CNN's "Sonya, Live" television show, wrote:

> Unfortunately, television is reality to many kids. It spells out how they see what's right and wrong. It is their parent, baby sitter and, in many situations, their only companion. Can we really believe that a lot of young women can make the distinction that Murphy Brown is fiction. . . .
>
> And why is Murphy having a baby, anyhow? Because her biological clock is running down? What kind of reason is that? *What happened to having babies because they were the concrete representation of the love between husband and wife?* (Emphasis added.)[2]

Barbara Whitehead, a research associate with the New York-based Institute for American Values, chimed in, too, saying:

> The plain truth is that every child needs both a mother and a father. A father cannot be replaced by a paycheck, or by a therapist, or even by Murphy Brown. In real life, fatherlessness wounds children, exposing them to a host of ills. If you want proof, turn on the evening news.[3]

In fact, while many stand-up comedians were having a field day at Quayle's expense, the evidence seemed to point to widespread agreement with him among the American people. Newspaper and radio polls showed support running anywhere from three-to-one in his favor to, in some cases, eight-to-one. And a Gallup poll released earlier in the month by the National Center for Fathering found that 70 percent of Americans agreed with the statement, "the most significant problem facing the American family is the physical absence of the father from the home." The consensus has not reached Hollywood yet but an increasing number of us are ready to give common sense its due.

What Works

All over the country heroic men and women are creating innovative approaches to address the needs of hurting and broken families. In Cleveland, Ohio former convict Charles Ballard is saving young men. Over a ten-year period, Ballard has put more than two thousand young fathers through his program. He insists that every participant do three things: (1) Take responsibility for the children they have fathered by marrying the mother or going to court and acknowledging their paternity, (2) stay in school or get a GED, and (3) find gainful employment "so you can learn responsibility and what it means to show up on time."

Ballard teaches these young men how to be fathers and responsible husbands, and then he recruits them to teach their peers the same values. His work is so effective that it has been described as "cloning miracles." In fact, Ballard himself is a miracle. He served eight months in prison, but while he was incarcerated he was brought to Christ by another inmate.

Many miles away, in Baltimore, Maryland, another dedicated man, Mark Shriver, runs the Choice Program. Mark and his staff are on call twenty-four hours a day to track and monitor the children, ranging from ten to seventeen, who are assigned to them. The Choice people bathe the children in attention. They check on them in school, on the streets, wherever they are. The Choice volunteers have no legal power, just moral authority. But because their children see them so much they have a lot of that built up. The Choice people work sixty to seventy hours a week. They get eight days off a year, and they are paid $17,500 a year. They do this, as one worker put it, to deal with three problems: "No values taught, no limits set, no consequences given."

The usually unemotional columnist George Will was so impressed by the Choice program that he found himself asking what was the secret of its success. He concluded the answer could be found on a poster in Shriver's office. The poster shows a small black child with the words: "God made me. God don't make junk."[4]

Rethinking Feminism

It may be that one of the best kept secrets of American life in the '90s is that radical feminism is dead. By feminism I don't mean the reasonable philosophy that seeks more equal economic and social opportunity for women. As the '90s progress, we will see new opportunities opening up for women in business, politics, and the arts. In the work place the gap in pay between men and women will narrow as more females have access to high-level jobs.

All of this is good and long overdue. It means that my daughters and yours will have a better chance to use their God-given talents. But the trend toward more economic opportunity has little to do with the radical brand of feminism that rejects family, motherhood, and marriage. I don't believe that feminism will ever be embraced by the majority of American women—and I believe that is a very good thing, too.

Liberal and feminist writer Sally Quinn summed up the trends in a column in the *Washington Post* that generated a lot of controversy. "The truth is," she wrote, "that many women have come to see the feminist movement as anti-male, anti-child, anti-family, anti-feminine. And therefore it has nothing to do with us."

Quinn was expressing a complaint that is being heard more and more frequently. A movement that started as a legitimate and long-overdue effort to gain fairness for women was somehow detoured by some of its radical leaders. Now it finds itself on a dead-end road. This peculiar brand of feminism sees all men as the enemy, marriage as a prison, and children as a liability. The editor of the leading feminist journal, *Ms.* magazine, has an editor who has gone so far as to assert that most of the "decently married bedrooms across America are settings for nightly rape."

Patricia Ireland, the new chairwoman of the National Organization for Women (NOW), whose husband lives in Miami, has publicly admitted she lives with a female "companion" in Washington, D.C. This "alternate lifestyle" was apparently fine with her husband, but it left many people wondering whether "leaders" like Ireland have anything in common with the values of most women. Incidentally, while some members of NOW expressed concern about the impact of Ireland's lifestyle, militants in the organization were outraged that she did not clearly and publicly commit herself to lesbianism.

Shortly after feminist leader and poet Erica Jong gave birth to her first child, she was invited to give a poetry reading in front of an audience of activists in the women's movement. Like most new mothers, Jong was overwhelmed with the emotion of bringing a new life into the world, and she chose to recite several poems expressing those feelings. She was shocked when the audience booed her off the stage. Jong has now become a critic of the feminist movement because of its hostility to mothering.

Fortunately, most women don't see men as "the enemy" or marriage as "a trap." Most women, with or without careers, want, sometime in their life, to be mothers. In fact, when American women were recently asked "What's the best thing about being a woman today?" 60 percent said motherhood. The second most popular choice was being a wife, and the third was "giving birth." Only after these traditional roles were mentioned did "increased opportunities" make the list. Most men and women in our country are searching for trust, love, and commitment. They yearn for a truce in the battle of the sexes.

Susan Faludi, in her best-selling book *Backlash,* charges that conservatism and a "conspiracy" of men are killing feminism. She then proceeds to argue, apparently with a straight face, that divorce doesn't impoverish women and that most women prefer working outside of the home instead of being home with their children. Finally, she argues that most thirty- and forty-something women without husbands really are very happy that they are living their lives alone. It is this type of radical world-view that is helping feminism commit suicide, separating it from most women.

A few years ago Gloria Steinem caused chuckles when she said, "A woman needs a man like a fish needs a bicycle," meaning not at all. It is a great line, but her point couldn't have been further from the truth. In the real world men and women need each other to share their lives together and to build a better future.

Unfortunately, radical feminism still thrives on some university campuses where captive students are fed a steady diet of this philosophy by "politically correct" professors. A few years ago when Barbara Bush was invited to speak at the Wellesley College commencement, a bevy of campus feminists objected. They were angry because Mrs. Bush had chosen to be a mother and homemaker rather than pursue her own career. She was the wrong role model for these "new" women.

The reaction of the public must have surprised the Wellesley ladies. Letters to the editor columns and radio talk shows were filled with expressions of support for the First Lady. It was a sign of healthy renewal. If feminism is about choice, young feminists should think twice about knocking the choice of nurturing a family. Americans care about family and about fidelity. They admire people, from the First Lady on down, who build their lives on these values.

The First Lady decided to use the controversy as a "teaching moment." In her address she urged the Wellesley graduates,

> to cherish your human connections: your relationships with friends and family. . . . As important as your obligations as a doctor, lawyer or business leader will be, you are a human being first and those human connections—with spouses, with children, with friends—are the most important investments you will ever make.

At the end of your life, you will never regret not having passed one more test, not winning one more verdict or not closing one more deal. You will regret time not spent with a husband, a friend, a child or a parent. . . .

Whatever the era . . . whatever the times, one thing will never change: Fathers and Mothers, if you have children . . . they must come first. You must read to your children, you must hug your children, you must love your children.

Your success as a family . . . our success as a society . . . depends *not* on what happens at the White House, but on what happens inside your house.

On the Street Where You Live

The family has been under pressure, but it is not breaking down as badly as the cultural elites would have us believe. There's a common sense way to do a reality check on all of the doomsaying family statistics. Is Pat Schroeder correct when she writes in her book, *The Great American Family,* that "traditional" families number only 7 percent of the population? The test is simple: Is this true in your own neighborhood?

Now, I would like to believe that the readers of this book represent a perfect cross section of the American people. Undoubtedly, that isn't true. But I've asked this same question of people I've met with in my travels and speeches in virtually every part of this great land. And the answer is, with few exceptions, categorical. Yes, there are problems—fractured families, families who are not fractured but hurting, separations of parent from parent and parents from children—but, on the whole, people say, "Families seem pretty much the same as they used to, it's the culture that's different."

Think about the Andersons three houses down. Dad is an accountant, very busy in tax season, seems to have a lot more time other parts of the years. Takes the kids to the park or makes dinner while Mom teaches class two nights a week at the junior college. Great family. But they're not traditional, according to Pat Schroeder's book, because Mom works, even if it's only part time. Or take the Brinkmoellers. Daughters Jamie and Chris are grown now. Chris is a junior at Ball State and Jamie is living with her former college roommate Shirley and working at Marshall-Fields as an assistant buyer. Neither the Brinkmoellers nor their children are "traditional" households according to one definition used by the U.S. Census Bureau, because Mom and Dad have no children living at home and their daughters are in group living arrangements.

The examples go on and on. For the Census Bureau, the distortion these definitions impart is hardly intentional. Only reading the fine print discovers them. For many anti-family radicals, however, the distortion seems to be part of an intentional campaign to ignore or eliminate traditional values generally. The combined effect of the publicity reports from these two sources—and dozens of others—is to create in many families a sense of isolation from the prevailing trends of the time. When they look around them, this is not what they see. When they open the paper or switch on the evening news, they see little else.

In fact, married mothers living with their husbands make up three-quarters of the "Mother with child under eighteen" population. Seventy percent of all Americans live in households headed by a married couple. Even these facts don't accurately reflect the commitment to traditional values in our society.

Where in the world did the experts get the idea that a mother working outside of the home precludes her commitment to traditional values? Millions of women work because their families can't pay their bills without a second income. These women often turn down promotions and fast-track career advancement for a very traditional reason: They want to be with their family. A 1989 *USA Today* poll found that the thing mothers disliked most about their current childcare situation is not the cost or the child-staff ratio but "missing big events in children's lives." The poll also found that 73 percent of all mothers say they would stay home with their children full time "if money were not an issue."

It is true that we have more instances of divorce (although these have peaked), more illegitimacy, and more mothers in the work force. But the great majority of us want the same things for ourselves and our children that Americans have always wanted. Most of us look for a husband or wife to spend our lives with. Most of us have children or want children as an affirmation of our love and our commitment to the future. Most of us want our kids to believe in honesty, trustworthiness, fidelity, and faith and to love the nation of their birth. The surface appearance of America's families in the '90s has changed from the '50s, but our hearts, desires, and fears remain pretty much the same. Most families endure. Most children are raised to responsible adulthood. Most of us avoid the siren song of the popular culture.

Value Rich

Imagine for some horrible reason you could not be with your children in the years when their lives would be directed and their values formed. Imagine that you had the choice of letting your children be raised by one of two couples. One would be wealthy with all of the material assets imaginable. Your child would live in a big house, wear the best clothes, and drive a "hot" car. But this family believes in moral relativism, is cynical about hard work, and believes you take what you can. Imagine the other couple had only modest means. Your children would wear hand-me-down clothes, share a bedroom with a sibling, have to work after school, and save for their own college educations. But this family believes in reliable standards of right and wrong and the Golden Rule, and faith is an integral part of their lives. Give this hypothetical choice to the average American family and I have no doubt, even in an era that is supposedly fixated on greed, that most of us would choose the "possession poor" but "value-rich" family. In fact, Gallup reports that 68 percent of us believe it is more important for families "to make some financial sacrifices so that one parent can stay home to raise the children" than "to have both parents working so the family can benefit from the highest possible income."

The tragedy is that this choice just isn't there for millions of families. The issue is not maximizing income, it is bringing in enough money to pay a mortgage, put food on the table, and provide for education and health care.

Culture

For a long time now American culture has taken an ugly turn. And American families have reacted to the mess by fleeing from it when that was possible. The controversy over the National Endowment for the Arts, and the stream of offensive work it has subsidized in recent years, is generally about this fact: Here was ugliness from which the American people could not run away.

We could not run away from it because it was ours. We had bought and paid for it with our hard-earned tax money. A name-plate or announcement card or catalog bearing the title of an agency created in our name, by our Congress, was affixed to this ugliness. Most of us did not rebel against this abuse because we despised art, but because we deeply cared about it. We recognized that we were being deprived by our own government of the best weapon we have against the tide of ugliness on television, in the cinema, and in the art galleries. The right to refuse to partake.

Such refusal is a powerful weapon indeed. Lately, I'm convinced, humankind has been forced to bear a great deal of reality. It would like to opt out of at least a little of the ugliness. Given the choice and the chance, Americans will gladly support raising a magnificent statue memorializing the flag raising on Iwo Jima, or the erection of our own Wailing Wall incised with the names of those Americans who were killed in Vietnam, but they want no part of the "porn art" that has made headlines recently.

How do I know this? Because time and again, the not-so-nice guys finish last. Movie critic Michael Medved pointed out in a recent article how disgusted the American public has become with Hollywood's output. He notes how a 1989 poll conducted by the Associated Press-Media General showed that 82 percent of Americans felt that the movies contained too much violence. Nearly as impressive majorities registered complaints about profanity and nudity in current films. Three-quarters of the public believed that, in terms of overall quality, movies were getting worse.[5] People are voting with their feet. According to figures reported in *Variety*, motion picture attendance in 1991 hit a fifteen-year low.

This is too large a segment to be constituted solely of the older generation of moviegoers who were brought up on classics like *Casablanca* or *Swing Time*, or even my generation that lined up for blocks to see movies like *Ben Hur* and *The Parent Trap*. The fact is, as Medved also points out, the top grossing films of the past decade have disproportionately included films released with ratings for general audiences. Story after story may be written about provocative films like *Henry and June* and *The Cook, the Thief, and His Lover* that push the outer limits of what is allowed, but the theaters are packed for movies like *Home Alone* and *Beauty and the Beast.*

The same is true for television where, I suspect, a poll might find that most Americans believe the trend is generally toward lower quality, too. When "The Cosby Show" left the air this year, it took with it plaudits as the top-ranked television program of the '80s. The series, which first aired in 1984, earned six Emmys and numerous other broadcasting awards. Focused on a black family, the Huxtables, the show shattered a number of shibboleths, portraying a strong, but far from conflict-free, intact family, with an obstetrician father and an attorney mother.

It was a favorite in the Bauer household, and my children were sorry to see the series end. When I served at the Department of Education I gave a speech suggesting that shows like "The Cosby Show" could do more for black children than a new government bureaucracy because of the values it taught. I still believe that to be the case.

Tradition and homespun values sell on television. Perhaps nothing proves this more than the public's reaction to the warm shows produced and presented on the Hallmark Hall of Fame. When Hallmark introduced Willa Cather's 1913 novel *O Pioneers* to a television audience, this wonderful tale of frontier life beat out *Indiana Jones and the Temple of Doom* in the ratings. Hallmark hit an Emmy jackpot with its production of *Sarah, Plain and Tall,* a story about a Kansas farmer who finds a mail-order wife to take care of his kids. They hit the jackpot again with their production of *Miss Rose White,* a moving story of a Polish immigrant who is reunited with her sister after World War II. My favorite in recent years was *Promise,* a touching story of a man (played by James Garner) taking care of his schizophrenic brother.[6]

What do these productions have in common? They deal with families and love, the commitments we have to each other, tradition, and the pull of hearth and home. These shows gained top ratings and critical acclaim. They kept millions of families riveted to their television screens and did it with no violence or overt sex. And Hallmark avoids like the plague the bizarre and warped themes we are so often exposed to during prime-time television, and viewers loved them for it.

Unfortunately, television still doesn't know how to handle religion. Neither does film, for the most part, although *Home Alone* included at least one scene played perfectly straight in a church, and exceptions like *Chariots of Fire* remind us of what we're missing. But while "The Cosby Show" has been criticized from the left for downplaying the effects of racism and by family advocates for its failure to portray the church life of its principals (almost a given for black families in America), the program's success stands as a testament to the fact that the vast majority of the nation's people identify with the family and treasure all its joys, humanity, humor, and pain.

I had similar thoughts during a recent fund-raising drive for the public television station in our area. Washington, D.C. prides itself on its sophistication and tolerance. When presidential candidate Pat Buchanan used scenes from a public-television-supported "documentary," *Tongues Untied,* in a campaign commercial in Georgia, more D.C.-based pundits expressed outrage at the "political" use of the issue than ever protested the original broadcast. *Tongues Untied,* an unfocused diatribe on homosexuality in the black community, had such offensive language and images that dozens of public television stations across the country refused to carry it. Many others broadcast it in a time slot once reserved solely for test patterns and the playing of the Star Spangled Banner.

But when the public television stations in the nation's capital appeal for donations, it is not their openness to broadcasting programs like *Tongues Untied* that they advertise. Instead, they rebroadcast impressive programs like "Anne of Green Gables," with Colleen Dewhurst; Miss Marple, Sherlock Holmes, and Hercule Poirot; retrospectives of Gene Kelly and Fred Astaire movies; the best of "Masterpiece Theater" and "Upstairs, Downstairs." They must know how idly the banks of volunteers would sit on screen if the fund-raising soliloquies were interrupted for images of militant homosexuals defending their attack on St. Patrick's Cathedral and attempting to villainize Cardinal O'Connor. Very few tote bags would move that night. Very few volunteers would come back for the pleasure.

If high-quality, mainstream programming is the fund-raising venue chosen by the public television channels in the nation's capital, that is even more likely to be the case elsewhere around the country. This is particularly interesting given the financial profile of those who donate to public television. About 5.2 million people give money to support public television nationwide. The average household income of donors to WETA, the flagship station in the Washington, D.C. area, is $94,583, about three times the median income of the nation as a whole. When WETA wants them to renew their support, they are shown Anne of Avonlea, not Annie Sprinkle. This is the type of program viewers want to believe they are making possible.

After National Endowment for the Arts chairman John Frohnmayer was dismissed from his post, he delivered a scathing speech at the National Press Club in Washington. He personally mocked critics of the NEA, adopting, at one point, a derisive Southern drawl to mimic the voice of the opposition. He repeated an argument that he used repeatedly during the controversy, that, of all the thousands of grants the NEA had awarded, a mere handful had caused any outrage. He pointed out that the NEA budget represents a contribution of less than $1 per citizen. One of the NEA grants went to help publish a book of poems called *Queer City*. One poem depicted Jesus Christ in an act of perversion with a six-year-old boy.

I've often wondered how public officials can misread issues so terribly. The average citizen does not want even a dollar of his own money spent on smut or to subsidize attacks on our most deeply held religious views. To the "big picture" bureaucrat, spending $15,000 in indirect subsidies on a performance by "post-porn" star Annie Sprinkle at New York's Kitchen Theater is just small change—hardly worth the fuss. But on Mulberry Street in Millersville and "Everytown," America, that $15,000 represents the total annual federal tax contribution of five median-income families of four. It's more than three times the total income any one of those families can shield from tax just to raise their children.

When government takes this sum of money away from any American family, it must have a very good reason for doing so. Officials who want to enjoy the public's trust must relearn to use the financial yardstick of Millersville, not of *Money* magazine. But if they are proud and insulated from the families they serve, this is unlikely to happen.

The market is a far from perfect barometer, or protector, of public sentiment. But the market does tell us a great deal about ourselves and about the deep-seated hunger that still exists in most people for a culture that honors traditions and values families. The phenomenon suggests at least one way to improve the cultural life of the nation, and that is to end the subsidies that force the unwanted attentions of these artistic nihilists on an entire nation.

Pornography

There are encouraging signs of progress in the struggle against pornography. Our own courts have long held that obscenity is not protected by the Constitution (someone better tell the American Civil Liberties Union). In early 1992 the Canadian Supreme Court upheld the obscenity provision in that nation's criminal code. Going even further, the Canadian Court decided that pornography was related to violence against women, and that when freedom of expression clashes with the right of women and children to be protected against violent sex crimes, the rights of women and children should come first.

The U.S. Justice Department began to prosecute hard-core obscenity more aggressively in the '80s. While the system moves slowly, after years in the courts, convictions of major pornographers are now coming through. Some pornographers, such as the notorious Reuben Sturman of Cleveland and Los Angeles, have pleaded guilty and are not only facing prison terms but also the loss of the financial fruits they accumulated through illegal activities.

In a free society it will always be difficult, if not impossible, to completely stop the production and distribution of obscene material. Laws help. We need to support legislation that attempts to stop the exploitation of women. But there is much we can do in our own homes with our own sons to teach them that material that treats women as toys for their pleasure is off limits even when, or if, it is legal.

All over the country men are beginning to stand up and deliver a strong anti-pornography message. A new ad campaign called "Real Men Don't Use Porn" is now being used in more than twenty states and seventy cities. It features prominent athletes and other male role models delivering a solid message against pornography. In Kansas City, a local citizen's organization, the Coalition Against Pornography, rented a billboard directly across the street from a hard-core adult bookstore.

Featured on the billboard were Storm Davis, then with the Kansas City Royals, and three former pro football players. The results were astonishing. Some customers of the X-rated store changed their buying habits after seeing the billboard.

Chris Cooper, the executive director of the Kansas City antiporn group, tells an even more encouraging story. He heard that a seven-year-old boy, Aaron, returned home from his uncle's house and told his mother, "Mom, Uncle Rich is not a real man. He had these bad magazines, and I had to turn them over." What a breakthrough it would be if all boys in America grew up thinking like that!

If America is to "go home" we must teach our sons the difference between love and sex. Fathers teach children in everything they do more so than by what they merely say. A child who sees his father treating his mother with love and respect is well on his way to becoming the kind of man who will treat women with respect and affection. A son who watches his father take pleasure in "reading" *Penthouse* and *Hustler* is unlikely to think of women as anything more than objects for his pleasure. In an era when the breakdown of sexual restraints has led to record levels of sex crimes, including rape and violence against women, there can be few things more important than teaching our sons to be "real men."

There is a clear and hopeful message in all of this. No matter how often the intelligentsia and the cultural elite tell us that the traditional family is dead, that men and women are alike, that nothing is always right or always wrong, that it's inevitable and OK for our children to have sex—average Americans just don't believe it.

To be sure, some of us were tempted by the Brave New World presented to us: sex without love, couplings without commitment, a new set of values each day, depending on the circumstances.

But the new philosophy failed at a basic level: It isn't true and it doesn't work. Those who went down the road away from hearth and home have paid a terrible price. The healing must begin now.

I Only Have Eyes for You

Abstinence is in. Even in Magic Johnson's fractured formula, "The best sex is no sex." The tragic announcement by the Los Angeles Lakers' star player that he carries HIV, the virus that causes AIDS, stunned millions of people around the world. Millions of words were written about his courage, his condition, his past, and his future. Speculation and rumor about how he contracted the virus abounded. Virtually everyone mentioned his promiscuous lifestyle on the NBA's superstar orbit. Virtually no one defended it, the first time in his entire career that this gifted basketball player was left unguarded.

Magic Johnson has gone on to disappoint many of us who deeply hoped he would become a real mentor to the young. Some other folks who, I believe, have wanted in their heart of hearts to display condoms to kids for decades, found in Magic a perfect excuse for fulfilling their wishes. Linda Ellerbee of the ineptly named Lucky Duck Productions pressed Magic into filming a special for broadcast on Nickelodeon, the children's channel. My blood boiled as I watched boys and girls from eight to fourteen years of age being subjected to an explicit demonstration of condom use and an appeal, spoken with all the knowing tenderness Captain Kangaroo once used to offer Bunny Rabbit a carrot, to deploy condoms to prevent HIV infection.

Just a few weeks before that program was aired, my good friend and colleague Dr. James Dobson, President of Focus on the Family, was asked to appear on an ABC special hosted by Peter Jennings. The program was supposed to present a balanced discussion of how to deal with the AIDS epidemic. In a ninety-minute program Dr. Dobson had ninety seconds to talk about abstinence. One other guest was able to support him briefly. The remaining eighty-eight minutes dealt with condoms, although in almost all of that time, little was said about what we now know, that relying on them is like playing Russian roulette.

For all their explicitness (as columnist Joe Sobran recently pointed out, the sex propagandists find a way to be explicit without ever being truthful), the proclamations of the condom educators have the brassy sound of a decaying empire. The emperors of eros desperately want their rule to continue, but parents know their Pied Piping threatens to deprive them of what they value most, the next generation.

No, Magic did not have it quite right, even when he had it best. The best sex is not "no sex," but "not yet" sex. Or as Nadine Bynum, a young woman who has worked with the minority community in Washington, D.C., puts it, "The best sex is saved sex." Saved for marriage, saved for that one person who will stand by you lifelong, saved for a lifetime of love and family. This is what most parents try to teach their children.

Magic has gone on to lend his name to a book on the subject. The education director for New York's Gay Men's Health Crisis describes the book, *What You Can Do to Avoid AIDS,* as a "fantastic resource." Whether or not it makes the bestseller lists, somehow I don't think the American people will really buy it. The book recommends an eight-step process to young people for using condoms and urges plenty of practice to help them keep the process straight—"boys on themselves, girls on vegetables," as one review put it.

When I was growing up, virtue consisted in helping young people realize the value of eating their vegetables. Despite the media and publishing magnates who are all too happy to have a figure of Magic Johnson's fame touting their wares, the consensus building around the abstinence message is too powerful for anyone to ignore. In time, as the condom comics and caped crusaders frolic off to futility, and the last bullet of the value-free crowd has been spent, this consensus will emerge with irresistible force.

It has already begun to do so, because the bottom line is that we are not in a game anymore. Children's lives are at stake, as is their chance for the friendship, fun, and fulfillment of marriage. As are their souls. Governor Doug Wilder of Virginia led off the liberal reawakening with a common-sense essay in the *Wall Street Journal* arguing that the very future of the black family depends on whether or not young blacks are taught to abstain:

> If they want to have a future, it is imperative that our young, male and female alike, embrace the ultimate precaution—abstinence. For as others have noted, "The essence of chastity is the total orientation of one's life toward a goal," and—in this instance—that goal must be a life of self-discipline, self-improvement and an abiding spirit of selflessness.[7]

The following summer, the National Commission on Children issued its final report and spoke in similar terms:

> Today too many young people seem adrift, without a steady moral compass to direct their daily behavior or to plot a thoughtful and responsible course for their lives. We see the worst manifestations of this in reports of violence and predatory behavior by adolescents in large and small communities across the nation. It is evident in lifestyles and sexual conduct that indulge personal gratification at the expense of others' safety and well-being.[8]

For most Americans, this is an elementary expression of the Golden Rule. But for government, this is a great leap forward indeed. Little more than a decade ago, a federally funded booklet aimed at teenagers included an interview with a physician associated with a Planned Parenthood agency in California that had used money from Uncle Sam to draft a model sex education curriculum for the entire nation. The doctor advised young people that having multiple sexual partners in and of itself had no implications for them.

> If . . . you have separated your sex and love needs and realize that a close relationship involves a lot more than just sex, and you're doing the sexual number for whatever reason—it interests you, it's fun, it's in keeping with your values, then you could have a hundred partners and still be a perfect candidate

> for a good close relationship later on. So having multiple sexual partners in itself doesn't mean anything."[9]

From coast to coast, in the afterglow of Woodstock and Haight-Asbury Street, advice like this to the young was all too common. It was foolish then, but after Magic and thousands of others, it's nothing less than criminal now. Again, the National Commission on Children's assessment was blunt: The sexual revolution is more like a sexual revolver, loaded for roulette. "Sexual activity," it noted, "especially with multiple partners, carries with it the risk of sexually transmitted diseases. . . . These diseases can cause serious, lasting health problems, including sterility."[10]

Judy Mann is a regular columnist for the *Washington Post,* and I usually find little to agree with in her columns. She has spent much of the past decade lambasting defenders of traditional values for seeking to impose their morality on others. In April 1992 the House Select Committee on Children, Youth, and Families, chaired by Congresswoman Pat Schroeder, published a report on teenagers and AIDS. Several members of the committee issued a powerful minority report arguing for abstinence as the only authentic measure to combat this plague. Much to my surprise and shock, Mann seemed to agree.

"Is there anyone," she wrote, "who would argue that a 12-, 13-, 14-, 15-, or 16-year-old child—yes, I said child—ought to be having sexual intercourse? Can we not all agree that, raging hormones or not, this is simply too young?" Mann then mentioned and rejected the taunt pro-family advocates nearly always hear when they offer this advice on the talk shows and in public debate, that teenagers won't listen. She said,

> But I'm not so sure of that. I hear young girls talking, and, frankly, they are saying some of the things women of my generation said. The difference? They are feeling the pressure to perform sexually at a much younger age than my generation did. The similarity? They don't like the pressure either.[11]

Young people are indeed asking for help in fighting off the pressure. The backlash today against date rape and sexual harassment represents an extension of this reaction against pressure among college-age and working women. They are an attempt to recover patterns of behavior that were once expected of everyone, not merely on the job site, but in the campus dorm and at the school dance.

Leon Kass, who teaches at the University of Chicago, caught the sense of that older, in fact, ancient code extremely well in a recent piece he wrote for *Commentary,* entitled "Regarding Daughters and Sisters." The main argument of his article was a masterful exploration of the meaning of the Old Testament story of Dinah, Jacob's daughter, and how Jacob's sons avenged her rape by the son of the Shechemite king.

But Kass went on to draw some keen conclusions about the damage done by the muse of sexual liberation. "The sexual revolution," he wrote,

> deliberately sacrificed female virtue on the altar of the god of pleasure now. Not surprisingly, the result was emancipated male predation and exploitation, as men were permitted easy conquests of women without responsibility or lasting intimacy. Unhappy with this outcome, but failing to appreciate its roots in the overthrow of modesty, the liberated women's movement mounted a moralistic political campaign against the "patriarchy," seeking power and respect, mistakenly believing that the respect women need as women is based solely on power.

They may reject Kass's language, but more and more feminist writers, radical and otherwise, are asking to be treated like ladies. Or pleading for their daughters to be. And there may lie the source of this explosion of common sense. It is a terrible spectacle to watch the cultural and commercial sexualization of children. It is ludicrous to think that training teenage girls to rehearse sexual encounters with condoms and cucumbers will help forestall male pressure or promote female resistance. It is more logical to believe that the young men, who have been "practicing" at home and who know the young women have been practicing too, will conclude that a little extra "pressure" on a date is expected and appropriate.

Mann holds out the hope that we can "line up all the various institutions that shape behavior of young people" behind the abstinence message. Alvin Pouissant, a psychiatrist at Harvard, notes how doing so will help the young people who don't want to say yes to sex, but feel that no one will back them up if they dare to be different. "This gives them a reason to say no," he argues. In the end, these teens must come to know that they really are not all that different, that, in fact, they are the working majority.

A week after Magic Johnson's revelation in November 1991, *USA Weekend* conducted a nationwide poll of teenagers and adults about the safe sex message. The poll found that the message troubles most people—and a higher percentage of teenagers than adults—because it can be construed to condone casual sex. A majority of young people felt that teens hear too little about chastity, another 32 percent said they hear enough about it, and only 12 percent said they hear too much.

Imagine that! Here are our children crying out to be told the value framework to help them avoid sexual relationships before marriage. The popular image of adolescents perpetually "in heat," unable to control themselves, and laughing at their parents' hangups, just isn't true. Many young people have witnessed firsthand the tragedy that comes with promiscuity. They desperately need our help.

Years ago parents could get away with avoiding the subjects of love and sex. These value-laden issues are never easy to talk over with children. But to fail to sit down with your children today, to arm them with the facts and a philosophy that enables them to defend virtue is unforgivable. Don't let strangers, bureaucrats, or rock stars teach your children about some of the most important issues they will face in their lives.

The National Commission on Children also believes children need to hear more about chastity. It closed its section on the adolescent years with a recommendation that Congress increase funding for abstinence education programs to $40 million annually (a bare $7.8 million is spent now). Of course, there are still a few degreed graduates of the abstinence-is-unrealistic school. Congresswoman Pat Schroeder failed, fortunately, in her attempt to wipe out all funding for the abstinence program during the 1991 floor debate in the House of Representatives. When I appeared before her select committee several months later and challenged her on this issue, she chose not to defend her actions but only to wonder out loud why I would be so "confrontational." But confrontation is desperately needed so that we can decide which way to go: further down into the muck of the sexual revolution or up to the lasting values that have sustained us and guided us on matters of love and sex for millennia.

Unfortunately, common sense and truth will probably come to Washington, D.C. and the federal bureaucracy only after they have been everywhere else. While condom distribution plans for school children make the headlines, in many communities around the country a "chastity revolution" is under way. New abstinence-based sex education programs like Sex Respect are gaining more adherents. Some cities and states have now passed laws requiring that children be told that abstaining until marriage is "the expected norm." Even in New York City, as we went to press, the school board was demanding (unfortunately, by a narrow one-vote margin) that the city's children be told as much about abstinence as they are about condoms. New York might even eventually learn that you can't have it both ways. Urging kids to abstain in one breath while passing out condoms in the next is unlikely to give our children a clear message of what is expected of them.

An innovative program developed by Maryland officials might be a hint of a new common-sense attitude. The state hired a Baltimore advertising agency to promote self-restraint. A typical message featured a picture of an infant with the words, "It's amazing how many guys disappear when one of these shows up."

State officials claim the results have been spectacular, and if the statistics are true, they are right. In 1989, the first year of the advertising campaign, the teenage pregnancy rate fell 5 percent and 6 percent more the following year. And the state's abortion rate fell 16 percent!

One newspaper was so enthusiastic when it saw the results that it came to a remarkable conclusion (for the '90s anyway): "No law of nature is forcing American teenagers into sexual relations. They can exercise self-restraint."

Sex Ed

In Illinois, Kathleen Sullivan has put together an acclaimed sex education curriculum that seeks to explain to young people why waiting is best. To preserve the natural sense of modesty, boys and girls are usually taught in separate classes.

In the boys' sessions an interesting and effective approach is used to help the young men focus on consequences. A rose is passed around the room from boy to boy—the rose symbolizing a young lady. Each boy is asked to imagine that he has convinced the young lady into going to bed with him. Each boy then removes a petal from the rose to symbolize what he has taken. As the rose is passed from boy to boy, the beautiful flower is soon transformed into a barren stem. When it reaches the last boy, the teacher comments, "Bob, meet your wife."

The exercise has its critics, of course. Anything that is done in the emotional area of love and sex involving young people will eventually ruffle someone's feathers. But I believe it is a highly effective way for these young men to be taught the consequences of their acts. Besides, if you are like me you are probably a little tired of the continual emphasis only on unmarried teenage *mothers* and promiscuous *girls*. These young women don't get miraculously pregnant all by themselves. There were teenage *fathers* involved and promiscuous *boys*. It is time we take responsibility for teaching our sons what real manhood is about, and it is time to make them meet their responsibilities when they fail to heed our advice.

The Fight Goes On

I don't mean to suggest that the battle over teaching about love and sex is over and the good guys have won. The decade of the '90s will likely determine the outcome and the fight will be bitter. Two world-views are clashing on this issue as on so many others involving what we will and should teach our children. Only one of them will prevail. If we truly want to go home, it should be painfully obvious by now that it can't be done if the sexual revolution, already devastating in its impact, is left unchecked. If more children succumb to the "pleasure now" siren song, and if latex is the best we can offer our sons and daughters in response to the physical and emotional dangers of early and promiscuous sexual activity, then our journey home is likely to end in a ditch, hopelessly mired in the mud that so many other civilizations have sunk and perished in.

Abstinence and reliable standards of right and wrong have a major advantage over the alternatives: They work while the other approach doesn't—as some communities are sadly finding out. Adams City High School in Commerce City, Colorado is known as a "progressive" school. It was one of the first schools in the country to start handing out condoms in 1989. Since 1979 the school has provided an in-house nursery for students' babies, counseling for student parents, and a course in parenting skills. Put it all together, and it is obvious that all the social censure for promiscuity and out-of-wedlock births was removed.

Not surprisingly, the results have been a disaster. In 1991, seventy-six Adams City students became teen mothers. In 1992, a hundred births were expected, a rate 31 percent above the national average.

Puzzled school officials are quoted as having few explanations for the climbing pregnancy rate. They publicly say that the "condom distribution is strictly for disease prevention." Privately, they continue to hope it will lower the pregnancy rate. They just don't get it. These "experts" have become partners in the bad behavior of the students they are responsible for. As long as that partnership continues, teen pregnancy rates and venereal disease will worsen.

What Now?

There is good news. In one area after another of American life we are beginning to rediscover the old truth. In the last two chapters I have tried to outline what some of the hopeful signs are. But much rebuilding remains to be done. The social decay that took decades to take place won't be corrected in a month or a year. But it might be corrected in a decade, if all of us resolve to do what we can to hasten the process. There are things we can do on the job and ways we can impact our neighbors. But the most important things are what we do as parents in our own homes. Let's look at the parenting agenda next.

5

What Every Parent Must Do

CHILD PSYCHOLOGIST DR. Urie Bronfenbrenner was once asked, "What is the key ingredient in the successful development of a human being?" Without hesitation he replied, "Someone, some adult, has to be crazy about the kids." We all know what he meant. Our children need 100 percent of us. I can't have one eye on the television and one eye on Sarah's homework. You can't "listen" to your children when you're still replaying in your mind the big staff meeting at work. Kids have great antennae. They know where they stand in our priorities.

Unfortunately, we now live in an age in which too many children have no adult in their lives who is crazy about them. Alarming headlines tell us about abandoned infants left in trash cans and helpless toddlers abused, burned, beaten, and sexually assaulted. The foster-care system is overwhelmed with an influx of abandoned children. In every urban center there are children staying alive on the streets by literally selling themselves to adults for sexual purposes. In other homes, kids come last, after finances and leisure time. But these headline-grabbing horrors should not blind us to a central fact of life. Most parents, of all races and economic groups, love their children and are committed to their well-being. We must and will come up with ways to deal with the tragic exceptions, but we must never forget they are exceptions.

Patrick M. Morley in his great advice book, *The Man in the Mirror,* tells a heart-wrenching story about an ill-fated Alaskan fishing trip. Some fishermen in a small seaplane found a secluded bay where they could fish. They had a great day of pulling in salmon and then returned to their plane late in the afternoon. Much to their surprise they found the aircraft high and dry because of the fluctuating tides. There was no choice but to wait until morning when incoming tides would make takeoff possible again.

The next morning, with the plane afloat, they started the engine and took to the air. Within minutes, however, the plane fell back into the sea. A leak in one of the pontoons let it fill up with water, and the extra weight caused the plane to crash.

The three adult fishermen survived the crash as did Mark, the twelve-year-old son of one of the fishermen. After praying, the four abandoned the sinking plane and began to swim toward shore, fighting the cold waters and a vicious riptide as they went. Two of the men, strong swimmers, reached shore exhausted. But looking back out onto the water they saw the father cradling his son in his arms as they were swept out to sea. The father could have made shore alone, but his son, much smaller, could not. He had decided to die with his son rather than leave him.[1]

This is a secret most of our kids don't know. We love them so much we would willingly die for them. As a former under secretary of education, I have had the opportunity to speak at dozens of high school graduations and before countless community groups. I often retell this moving story. The students are fascinated by this act of heroism. They find it almost inconceivable. Then I ask each parent in the audience to raise his or her hand if they would be willing to lay down their lives for their children. Within seconds, every hand is raised as the astonished young people look around the room. It is always an emotional moment. For many I think it is the first time that they realize the depth of the love their parents feel for them.

Fortunately, of course, most of us will never have to literally die for our children. But in some ways we are required to do something even more challenging—to live for them. Having children today is a profound act of courage. It means bringing them into a world whose temptations abound, and it is clearly tougher to protect them than it used to be in simpler times in our nation.

Children cost a bundle to raise, as the Commerce Department reminds us every year. Of course, none of us needs a government agency to tell us what we already know by merely looking at our depleted checking accounts. Our childless friends generally have better houses, longer vacations, more fashionable clothes, and more discretionary income than we do. Educational costs alone are astronomical! (Financial planners tell us that if we would just put $100 aside each month after the birth of a child, education costs would be taken care of. They fail to take into consideration that many hard-pressed families with two or three children would do anything to have an extra $100 a month left over after doctor bills, braces, swimming lessons, and groceries.)

The world around us is a minefield. Parents find themselves in a constant battle with competing "spheres of influence," from the ever-present peer pressure to the popular culture of MTV, movies, and rock stars. Kids have become a "market" today. Everyone, from MTV to corporate giants, tries to sell our children products, and in the process they sell them something else—values—often at conflict with the values we teach at home. Parents feel as if they are in a tug of war with some pretty hefty opponents pulling against them. Then, after years of struggle, if you avoid disaster, your children leave you anyway. This exciting thought hit our oldest daughter, Elyse, one evening recently as the family was relaxing in the den after a hard day at work and school. With her youthful enthusiasm, she blurted out to her mother and me, "Wow, in four more years I will go away to college." My wife's reaction was swift; she immediately began to cry and ran out of the room. The rest of the evening was interesting, to say the least, as I tried to negotiate the treacherous ground between mother and daughter.

But in spite of all these "rational" arguments against childbearing, we continue to bring babies into the world. In fact, as we enter the '90s, the country is in the middle of a mini baby boom not expected by the experts. The instinctive desire to propagate the species is strong, of course, and this no doubt plays a role. But I believe that most of us know in our hearts that having a child and raising that son or daughter to responsible adulthood is likely to be the most profound and important thing we ever do.

As Time Goes By

I have found over the years that if you want to know about what's going on in the life of a family, there is a simple way of doing it—go to their refrigerator! I don't mean look inside to examine the food. Rather, examine the evidence of family life displayed on the outside.

At our house, and I suspect yours too, what's hanging on the refrigerator secured by those little magnets and scotch tape is a chronicle of the life of the family. Zachary's drawings of stick people, the girl's best homework papers, report cards, photos of relatives out of town but not out of mind, favorite Bible verses and homespun wisdom, plus a few menus from our favorite weekend carry-out eateries.

I recently talked to a reporter friend who was bemoaning the changes on the outside of his refrigerator. His "baby," the last of his three children, had just graduated from college. She had come home, and he had come upon her in the kitchen taking down her college phone number from the fridge and replacing it with her new work phone number.

Suddenly it struck him how the refrigerator had changed. The drawings were gone, as were the newspaper articles with mentions of childhood honors. A page had turned. I reminded him that if he were lucky, a whole new refrigerator chapter would begin—once a few grandchildren came along.

This reporter and his wife are both well-known press commentators. They move in important circles and analyze the events of the day. They debate the great issues on television and in the newsmagazines and critique presidents. But as I listened to this man talk about the joys of family life and how much he was missing the pleasures of having children around the house, I was reminded again of the power of hearth and home and its universal appeal.

Our children connect us to the future. They are daily reminders that life is sweetest when it is being lived for someone else. In them we see a reflection of ourselves for better or for worse. Our children are evidence of the love we share as husbands and wives. In their miraculous creation, there is also evidence that our lives are not the result of a cosmic accident, but instead the intentional will of God. They are, in fact, His children, "masterpieces from the very beginning," as the hit vocalist Sandi Patti so aptly puts it.

Everyday it becomes more evident to me that my happiness is tied to my children's. I never could understand the emotion I used to see displayed by parents on the sidelines at youthful sporting events, that is, until I had children myself. When Elyse fell off the balance beam at a gymnastic meet, I hurt just as if it were my own rump that had hit the ground. When our budding writer, Sarah, gets a "great work" note taped on an essay from her teacher, it's my chest that expands a couple of inches with pride. When Zach scores a soccer goal to win the game my heart leaps; when he fails, I'm pained, too.

Parents will do anything to protect their children. They often begin by trying to put the fear of God in them: "If you cross the street without looking, Mary, you'll get hit by a car . . . or wish you had." The other fear they work on is the healthy fear of strangers. One mother told me this story:

> When our little boy turned three and already had that gleam in his eye about running away to join the Foreign Legion, I gave him the same talk his older sisters got. This time my eight-year-old was listening in. "You know, son, if you don't stay in the yard, a bad man will see you. He'll offer you candy. When he gets you in the car, he'll take you away and you'll never see us again."

When I'd finished my speech, the eight-year-old put her face down close to his and, just to make sure he wasn't thinking it over, chimed in, "Yeah, and you still won't even get the candy."

Parents know their children are targets. Not merely of thieves and molesters, of whom there are relatively few, but of marketeers and shysters, of whom there are many. What most parents probably don't appreciate is how sophisticated and exact a science marketing to children has become. If God knows when every sparrow falls and the number of hairs on every human head, the merchants of Hollywood and Wall Street know how many coins jingle in a child's pocket . . . and how to get them.

A recent article in *American Demographics*, a monthly magazine charting trends of interest to U.S. business, discussed the "littlest shoppers," and the steps industry can take to attract the purchasing power of children, both the money they spend directly and the parental spending they influence. The article estimated that child-influenced expenditures in the United States total some $132 billion annually, more than the entire gross national product of Taiwan, one of the world's most successful economies.

You will have little trouble guessing the two commodities young people purchase most (especially if you consider what today's rock stars and athletes are most likely to be found advertising): soft drinks and fast food. Movies and music also come in for a large chunk of the teenage and pre-teen market. Apart from being a sign of affluence, America's youth market sometimes resembles a wasteland of developmental inappropriateness. To many parents it is not a case of "too much, too soon," as "not this, not ever."

Even when the material itself is not commercial, but only the interest in conveying it—as in television news—a sense of irresponsibility sometimes prevails. After the Clarence Thomas-Anita Hill hearings had played out, the local press carried reports of an anxious attorney who frantically phoned her husband's office mid-afternoon that Friday and begged him to hurry home and commandeer the television set lest their children tune in CNN after school. Allegations of sexual harassment at the EEOC threatened to become sexual harassment of latchkey children at home. Over-the-horizon parenting is clearly a difficult job.

Historian Daniel Boorstin has pointed out how in rural nineteenth-century America, the chief texts for child education were the Bible and the Sears catalog. For many decades the reading list expanded but the sense of children as a special class of customers, independent of their parents' values and desires, scarcely occurred to anyone.

Suppose, for example, it is the summer of 1951 and a traveling salesman appears at your front door. He carries a sample case and some unlabeled boxes. When the mother or father answers the door, he greets them with his "smile and a shoeshine," and asks if the "children of the house" are at home. He will not offer a sample or say what is in the boxes. "If the lady of the house will just let me talk to Jimmy and Susie, I won't take but a minute," he says. Would he have gotten a foot in the door? Even a chance to spill his ashes on the carpet? Would any salesman have even tried this approach in 1951?

Today this vignette may strike some as a little silly when the average American high school senior watches at least three hours of television a day, when millions of schoolchildren in the suburbs buy Guns n' Roses albums, and big-city teens commune with Two Live Crew. Several years ago when the Parents Music Resource Center was formed and began alerting parents to the violent, morbid, and sexually explicit content of rap and rock lyrics (a word that has wandered a long way from its etymological roots), the resistance from many performers was intense. Musician Frank Zappa waxed poetic about the First Amendment because parents merely wanted to know what was in the "box."

Probably the last thing that most parents wanted to do was begin listening intently to what their children were hearing. When they did so, and it wasn't "Teen Angel," a corner was quietly being turned. Labeling records has now become an established standard in the industry, and the truth is that even this modest step would not have happened without the persistent pressure of parents. The modern merchant no longer needs to knock on the front door. Radio and television let him in unbidden, checkered coat, straw hat, and all. But parents now know that if they pull together and stay unimpressed with the pitchman's spiel on constitutional law, they can keep some of the worst excesses in check.

Time

Each new generation presents the opportunity to reteach the values of hearth and home. It is harder today, to be sure. The popular culture appeals directly to our children over our heads. Peer pressure is stronger than ever and directed to ever more variations on the seven deadly sins. But children today, as always, are hungry for direction and guidance. Most of them, whether they ever say so or not, treasure forever the times when they receive it.

I've lived in Washington long enough to be inured to the overload of opinion surveys, but bear with me for just one more. A group of college students was asked about the family experiences they remembered and valued most. Only a handful cited vacations or other family events that required a lot of planning and execution. Trips to amusement parks, to the beach, or to museums came nowhere near topping the list. Instead, the students listed events that many families would hardly consider "events" at all: a conversation with a parent, a shared project around the house, or even something as simple as a running joke.

The bottom line is that our children need us. The world has changed a lot, but that basic fact hasn't. Kids tend to remind us of this truth even when we don't expect it. Not long ago I testified before the House Select Committee on Children, Youth, and Families. The committee chairwoman had arranged for a twelve-year-old kid who plays on a Nickelodeon television show to appear as one of its "star" witnesses. The idea was to use this child actor's appearance before this congressional panel to attract media attention and give some members of the committee and their carefully coached twelve-year-old accomplice a chance to call for "children's rights," more day care, and other "progressive" ideas that the experts in Washington think will solve our problems.

But Congressman Clyde Holloway rained on the committee's parade that day. With the cameras rolling and the packed hearing room hanging on each word, the Louisiana Republican turned to the twelve-year-old boy and asked, "If you could be king for a day, how would you spend your time?"

Caught off-guard by this unscripted inquiry, the child actor did a funny thing. With refreshing candor, he answered as I suspect most kids would. He said if he were king for a day, he'd want to spend his day at Disney World or at some other location filled with childhood amusements. He'd want to eat lots of ice cream and candy and stay up late. But most of all, he said he'd want to spend his day with his family, with his Mom and Dad, because between their busy work schedules, they never really spent enough time together.

For the last quarter-century, we have withstood an onslaught of garbage about "Supermoms" and irrelevant fathers and "quality time." But now, as the baby boomers finally begin to fill their quivers with children, America is coming home. It is leaving the whines of the anti-child radicals to respond to the whimpers of precious little children. As long as we listen to the mouths of babes, as long as we heed the cries of our children—who like that twelve-year-old yearn for us to invest our time in the eternal creatures God has entrusted to our care—we will all be like kings until we breathe our last breath.

Quality Time

I realize more than ever how illusive the old debate about quality vs. quantity time with children really was. The first mistake lay in thinking you could accurately define "quality" time.

From a child's point of view, this was probably nigh well impossible. Getting into "quality time" with another human being, adult or child, is like diving into an unheated pool in late April. An awful lot of transition time, not only for the harried adult but for the distracted child, must pass before the "water temperature" is right. A lot of doing nothing is needed before you can do something.

Many a parent has put a lot of chips on a long family vacation or a trip to Disneyland to strengthen bonds with a child or to make up for lost time. Such events can provide a host of happy memories for a family, but at their best they're no closer to the main course than an after-dinner mint. A wife in our circle of friends once told Carol and me about her most vivid memory of her father, dead now nearly twenty years. It was an everyday sight. "I can still see him, kneeling down in his work clothes at the end of a long day, leading our family in prayer."

Creating Memories

It is astonishing how home can create memories and give significance to sounds and sights that mean little to others who have not experienced their power. I once read of a Mississippi family who sent their military son in Korea a tape—not of voices but of something the son missed hearing—the booming thunder that accompanies summer rainstorms in the South. While growing up, the boy and his father used to stretch out on the floor and listen to it, the father laughing with each boom to keep his son from being afraid.

Weeks later after the soldier had received the tape, he called home. "Dad, you won't believe what I did last night. I invited some friends over to my quarters for a thunder party. When we heard the tape we all reacted the same way. Instant silence followed by a few minutes of sadness. But once we realized we were listening to the sounds of home, we felt better and enjoyed a great party, like we'd been relieved of a heavy burden. I can't tell you how much that tape meant to me."[2]

When I was growing up, my father and I would escape the un-air-conditioned house and sit on the old wooden back steps. There we would watch the yard come alive with fireflies, and he would point out the big dipper in the sky overhead. Now every firefly reminds me of those nights with Dad, and when I point out the dipper in the night sky to my children, my mind fills with the memories of those days a long time ago when pleasure could be found on a hot summer night merely sitting and watching with my father.

Then there were our fishing trips. There was nothing fancy about them either. The family would get up early on a Saturday, and my father and I would go down the street to the "bait man's" house. We'd buy some night crawlers and minnows and head out to a lake a few miles outside of town. It was stocked with a Kentucky favorite—catfish—and we'd spend hours trying to catch the "big one." We reeled in a few, but what I remember most are those long, hot afternoons, just sitting on the bank under a big shade tree, drinking a soda, and talking about small things. I remember baiting a hook with a squirming worm, sunburns, mosquito bites, and the aroma of fish and hamburgers on the grill.

I've had more exciting (and more expensive) fishing trips since, including deep-sea fishing in the Atlantic off the coast of Delaware. But none of the experiences since have matched those childhood days at the lake on a Saturday afternoon.

I don't know if my parents realized at the time that I would remember those fishing outings so fondly. I doubt it. It wasn't even clear to me what the trips would come to mean later. It was just a real nice way for a blue-collar family to have some cheap fun together.

What things will my own children remember about their years at home? For Zachary it might be our "bear hunting" trips in a wooded park just a half-mile from our house. There are no real bears there, of course, but with a youthful imagination and my encouragement, you would be surprised at how many "wild things" can almost be seen in the brush. Joggers run and frisbees sail through the air just yards away from us, but for Zachary we might as well be in the wilds of Africa.

In this frenzied world, it is more important than ever for parents to engage in inactivities with their children. That isn't a misprint. Inactivity, silence, "downtime." These are crucial to bringing out the depth that exists in any human being.

A good television program is a great pleasure. But a roomful of people watching television may be missing a lot. More young adults have probably seen "Homefront," a drama about life in the United States after World War II, than have ever spent an hour talking with their parents about what their lives were really like after the war. Regular silence in the home—clearing the decks—is crucial if we're to enjoy the kinds of communication summoned from the depth of experience that any family can and should be able to claim as its own.

Failing to spend time with our children is a mistake we are not likely to ever be able to make fully right. In 1988 an Ann Landers column described the anguish felt by a father who had let the precious years with his own children pass away.

> I remember talking to my friend a number of years ago about our children. Mine were 5 and 7 then, just the ages when their daddy means everything to them. I wished that I could have spent more time with my kids but I was too busy working. After all, I wanted to give them all the things I never had when I was growing up.
>
> I loved the idea of coming home and having them sit on my lap and tell me about their day. Unfortunately, most days I came home so late that I was only able to kiss them good night after they had gone to sleep.
>
> It is amazing how fast kids grow. Before I knew it, they were 9 and 11. I missed seeing them in school plays. Everyone said they were terrific, but the plays always seemed to go on when I was traveling for business or tied up in a special conference. The kids never complained, but I could see the disappointment in their eyes.
>
> I kept promising that I would have more time "next year." But the higher up the corporate ladder I climbed, the less time there seemed to be.

Suddenly they were no longer 9 and 11. They were 14 and 16. Teen-agers. I didn't see my daughter the night she went out on her first date or my son's championship basketball game. Mom made excuses and I managed to telephone and talk to them before they left the house. I could hear the disappointment in their voices, but I explained as best I could.

Don't ask where the years have gone. Those little kids are 19 and 21 now and in college. I can't believe it. My job is less demanding and I finally have time for them. But they have their own interests and there is no time for me. To be perfectly honest, I'm a little hurt.

It seems like yesterday that they were 5 and 7. I'd give anything to live those years over. You can bet your life I'd do it differently. But they are gone now, and so is my chance to be a real dad.

Education

Learning, too, is a matter of quantity as well as quality time. A SAT prep course may help, but if that is the foundation and not the penthouse, the building will fall. Children who successfully acquire real learning will have at their mental command the basic building blocks upon which the educational edifice rests. There is more need for a national consensus on these building blocks than there is for any national curriculum or eight-part plan to save America's schools.

I believe the consensus that parents must be deeply involved in the education of their children is now being slowly but surely restored. The National Commission on Children, which delivered its report in 1991, was quite specific about the extent of the parental role, and it is not a limited one. "Schools," it wrote, "should encourage and facilitate parent participation in governance and management processes and in school activities."[3] Besides providing a powerful argument for parental choice in education—if parents are fit to help manage schools, it is absurd to suggest they are incompetent to choose them—the commission's recommendations imply something more profound about the parental role, that is, it is irreplaceable.

The same message is emanating from the Progressive Policy Institute, a Washington-based think tank established by the Democratic Leadership Council, a group of moderate and conservative Democrats. "Government cannot replace the family," authors Elaine Kamarck and William Galston say in the 1990 report *Putting Families First,* "and it should not even try."

Parents who often feel, or are made to feel, like trespassers on school grounds, should take heart from these statements. Popular culture has not yet swung back to offering a positive image of parents who "weigh in" on issues affecting the education of their children. Cries of censorship or interference will often still greet them. But the first thing that any parent must do in today's environment is to recognize that his or her authority and experience do matter. Parents do make a difference.

Parental authority also is not confined to the home. It matters in the schools and on the streets. James Coleman, the well-known sociologist at the University of Chicago, suggested in a recent paper prepared for the Department of Education that parental involvement in young people's lives should be considered a form of "social capital"[4]—that, like capital, it should be accumulated and wisely invested. This no doubt comes as grim news to the American Civil Liberties Union and the tiny, but widely published legion of child liberators, who have struggled to push parents to the legal and social periphery of their children's lives.

Thus the first thing that parents must do is to reacquire their confidence. The baby they bring home from the hospital, stamped FRAGILE all over and that Dad is afraid to hold because it isn't labeled anywhere THIS SIDE UP, is a lot tougher than it first seems. As that baby grows and its needs become more complicated, the vast majority of parents grow right along with the child. With love and discipline, time and patience, they negotiate together the shoals of late childhood and adolescence—"adult lessons," as an eight-year-old acquaintance of mine once pronounced it.

Parenting is a task that more than 90 percent of men and women assume in virtually every generation. It has been done by princes and paupers, and typically done better by the latter. Even today when the marriage rate among young adults has declined and the median age at first marriage has risen by four years for brides (five years for grooms), the percentage of adults who marry at some point in their lives has not decreased appreciably. Marrying and having children is, after all, natural. How many advisory committees do you see around a robin's nest?

The essential tasks of parenting do not change. They are to provide shelter and nutrition, a *sense* of shelter and security, and a training ground to prepare the young for the responsibilities of that "office" called adulthood. It should have been elementary good sense (and for many centuries it was) that children, in order to grow up well and to perform the tasks of adulthood, relating successfully as a man or woman with both men *and* women, should have one of each in the home to guide and prepare them.

America's Smallest School . . . the Family

That was the title of a recent report by the Educational Testing Service. Finally, the experts are conceding what most of us knew already. Education, like charity, begins at home. Unfortunately, many parents have retreated from involvement in the educational enterprise. A recent study of thirteen hundred high school juniors and seniors showed that only 14 percent of the students felt that their parents were "heavily involved" in their schooling. The National Association of Secondary School Principals that conducted the survey said, "Judging from the responses, children have given parents a 'D' in involvement."

Parents, then, must get right back in the thick of things. Children will benefit by just seeing their parents willing to take part in school and community life, to serve, and, if necessary, to dissent and to stand their ground. It's difficult to do the unpopular thing. Peer pressure affects adults, too. But there is no better way for parents to demonstrate the value of independence to the young than by demonstrating it reasonably and firmly themselves.

Dissent is as American as apple pie, and certainly as American as compulsory school attendance. As Shakespeare's Henry V expressed it, "Every subject's duty is the king's, but every subject's soul is his own." The Book of Nehemiah says, "Remember the Lord who is great and awesome, and fight for your brothers, your sons and your daughters, your wives and your homes."

Naturally, I receive a lot of letters from parents who have approached their teacher or school board about some book or text they believe their child should not be exposed to, either in the classroom or the school library. The context is usually a sex education course, but occasionally it is a reading series or a literature class.

Each year Norman Lear's People for the American Way publishes a report on censorship in the schools, listing incidents where parents have challenged the suitability of a classroom text or library book. The list includes some sporadic incidents—a challenge to *Huckleberry Finn* by black parents in Chicago, for example—and some "repeat offenders" who regularly catch parents' ire, like Judy Blume and J. D. Salinger.

Frankly, People for the American Way has it all wrong, even on those few occasions when they're right about a particular book or film. The problem is not too much parental "interference," but too little. An eminent American poet once wrote that the entire function of a critic was to tell the reader what books he ought to read if for no other reason than to spare readers wasted time and money. The teacher of reading or literature is also a critic. So, too, is the interested parent.

It is hardly censorship to guide children to the very best in books and music, any more than it is "nutritional repression" to deny them chocolate cake in the school breakfast program. The parent who objects to the age appropriateness, tastefulness, or intelligence of a particular choice of texts is doing exactly what an effective parent must do. Teachers must be willing to defend their choices or to change them. They are the last people who ought to shun a debate, or to avoid what could be a "teaching moment."

Our schools must welcome parental activism. Even when the parent is wrong, it is clear that the parent cares. And often the parent is right, even in judgments about matters that are expressly the teacher's field. The fact of the matter is that as the general educational level of the populace rises, there are likely to be more conflicts about curricula and textbooks, not fewer. Parents often do know more. High school graduation rates that stood at 53 and 24 percent for whites and blacks, respectively, in 1950 stand at 86 and 82 percent today. Similar increases in college graduation rates have occurred. Moreover, their judgment is worthwhile and should ordinarily prevail, even when they know less, because of their role as parents.

Several years ago in Chicago, a group of black parents objected to the inclusion of *Huckleberry Finn* in a high school English course because of Twain's inclusion of an ugly racial epithet in reference to Huck's companion, the runaway slave, Jim. The parental sensitivities this controversy brought to the surface were better off not submerged. The conflict could, and perhaps did, bring forth a deeper understanding of both those sensitivities and of Twain's anti-slavery purposes (he calls slavery a "bald, grotesque, and unwarrantable usurpation"[5] in his autobiography) in writing the tale of Huck and Jim's extraordinary friendship.

James Coleman notes that conflicts of this kind have been "most prominent when communities and families were strong,"[6] not merely where a bastion of conservatism exists. Good educators will never want to see the day when they have their way unchallenged with the young people in their tutelage, or when the school has taken on all of the functions the family once fulfilled. That will be the day when the home has collapsed, the community is unsafe, and many children do not live long enough or avoid jail long enough to discover all of the wonderful variety their school might have offered them.

The Little Things

During my years in Washington I have had some unforgettable experiences. I had prime office space in the West Wing of the White House. On Mondays I joined a select group of top aides to have lunch with the president. I have flown on Air Force One and ridden in the president's motorcade through the streets of the nation's capital while police closed the intersections to traffic for our convenience. At cabinet meetings I argued and debated the issues facing our nation with the top leadership of the government. I've been on "Good Morning America," "Nightline," and all of the other top television news shows. Pretty heady stuff for a blue-collar kid from an Ohio river mill town.

It would strain credibility to suggest these things don't matter to me. I have devoted a significant amount of time and energy to influencing government policy to make it more "family friendly." But at night, after a hard day of work, with the lights low and the house quiet, I am not thinking about the corridors of power. Instead my thoughts return to my children, Zachary's cry of "let's wrestle" when I come home each night, my oldest daughter Elyse as she is transformed into a young woman, bubbly Sarah and her vivid imagination. I think about the love of my wife Carol, of the first tiny, one-bedroom apartment we shared as newlyweds, the budget books where every dime was recorded so we could save for our first house, of the struggles, victories, and defeats we have shared.

I'm not unique. This is what most of us cherish. Most of us realize that real happiness is at home. For most Americans life is not about possessions, power, or clout. It is helping hands and good neighbors, nighttime prayers and lovingly packed lunchboxes. It is hard work and a little put away for the future. No government would ever command those things. And as Washington is tragically finding out, no government can duplicate them. They are done naturally out of love and a commitment to the future.

Good Family Man

Do you remember when the highest compliment that could be paid to an adult male was, "He's a good family man"? David Blankenhorn of the Institute for American Values has pointed out that our culture no longer celebrates the ideal of the man who puts his family first. David is a great analyst of the contemporary scene, but I fear he may be unduly influenced by the culture in New York City.

In fact, I believe there is growing evidence that men are finding that the greatest and most satisfying thing they can do is be a loving father and husband. Certainly those in our culture who argued that women and children don't need men have been proven wrong on this question as on other social trends. Our most desperate communities are those where "good family men" are nowhere to be found. In these communities impoverished women and their children have merely Uncle Sam and a list of federal programs to help them. It doesn't work.

Clubhouse magazine, a publication of James Dobson's Focus on the Family, recently asked its young readers to share what they liked most about their dad. Responses poured in and almost every one was a gem. I was struck by how seldom these children mentioned physical possessions or material things their fathers provided them. Instead it was the simple manifestations of love and commitment that were cited most often, the very things that sometimes fall by the wayside in our increasingly fast-moving world.

> "A father should be not only your dad, but your friend, too"—Samantha, age ten, Southaven, Mississippi
>
> "My dad's most important quality is his willingness to ask forgiveness from me when he is wrong"—Stephanie, age nine, Duluth, Georgia
>
> "A good dad would come to your games . . . and miss work just for you"—Brook, age twelve, Roswell, Georgia

> "The most important quality in my father is that he makes me feel safe"—Erin, age nine, Kansas City, Missouri
>
> "A dad must discipline you when you do something wrong so you won't grow up to be a bad person"—Lisa, age thirteen, Concord, California
>
> "I think a dad should care about his children's grades and their lives. And it helps when your dad will study for a test with you"—Lynn, age ten, Chambersburg, Pennsylvania
>
> "The most important qualities of a father are that he loves and does the best he can for his kids. My dad does that all the time . . . well, most of the time. No dad is perfect"—Alicia, age eleven, Wausaw, Wisconsin

All of these touched my heart. But one came at me like a freight train. It was written by ten-year-old Sommer from Fergus Falls, Minnesota: "The most important thing is that my father loves my mother."

Our children do need our time and attention. They need us to overcome their fears and to help them dream dreams. But they also need to know that as parents we love each other. And in an age when an increasing number of men have headed for the hills they need to see clearly the unhedged love we have for their mothers.

Full-time homemakers are one of the least appreciated segments of our population. Sylvia Porter, the noted financial analyst, has calculated that our nation's 25 million homemakers contribute billions to the economy each year. She found that the labor provided by a mother at home would cost $23,580 in Greensboro, South Carolina; $26,962 in Los Angeles; and $28,735 in Chicago. Even these estimates are low since they were based on assigning an hourly wage scale to duties such as cook, chauffeur, dietician, and practical nurse. What would the real figure be if monetary value were assigned to high-status jobs that every mother performs out of love: teacher, child psychologist, and religious instructor, for example?

Porter's conclusion, "Your government should give you a medal for productivity. Your family should appreciate and cherish you."[7] The best way for our children to be taught to appreciate their mothers is for them to see their fathers appreciate them. In today's world which breeds insecurity, our children need to be reassured of the love their parents have for each other.

6

What Every Child Should Be Taught

A CROSBY, STILLS AND NASH tune that was popular in the turbulent '70s urged parents to "teach, teach your children well." They were great vocalists, but they were hardly the first with that advice. A much older Proverb said it far better: "Train up a child in the way he should go and when he is old he will not depart from it." But the questions have always been, "Teach them what?" "What way should our children go?" "How do we teach them well?"

Perhaps we should begin by reminding ourselves what we should *not* teach. At the top of that list is moral relativism, unfortunately the prevailing philosophy in our culture for a long time now. Simply understood, moral relativism says, "People can do whatever they want, without regard to any universal standards." It is not hard to see why young people, who tend to focus on life today while only dimly seeing the consequences tomorrow, would find this philosophy attractive. Professor Christina Hoff Sommers of Clark University has bemoaned the fact that many students come out of college ethics courses having learned that "there is no such thing as morality." One "enlightened" graduate put it this way: "I learned there is no such thing as right or wrong, just good and bad arguments." Imagine how you would feel as a parent, working, sacrificing, and saving tuition money for years and then having that as the philosophy of life your child received from a so-called higher education. The student or his parents would be justified to demand a refund for educational malpractice!

The failure of moral relativism is painfully evident to nearly everyone by now. This empty philosophy has contributed in a major way to the destruction, decay, and tragedy of the last thirty years. But it is not enough for us to merely reject what has not worked. There are positive lessons of life we have an obligation to teach our children if our nation is going to recapture the values of heart and home. The Massachusetts Mutual survey that I described earlier found that most of us know instinctively that home is the place where we learn the most central truths about life and love. We can't leave it to the popular culture, MTV, and the unreal and surreal worlds of television and Hollywood to take the responsibility of teaching our children away from us.

Different Strokes for Different Folks

America is a much more pluralistic society than it was twenty or thirty years ago. Different traditions will and should prevail in some households reflecting the particular cultural heritage of the family. But that pluralism doesn't mean we must be paralyzed when it comes to finding a values consensus. There are universal values that transcend racial, social, and economic differences. There is a common heritage that we share as free men and women, and that heritage must be passed on. History teaches us lessons about the right way to live, and those lessons are equally relevant to all of our children whether they live in the inner city, the suburbs, or in rural America. No society can ultimately be value neutral.

When pornography that exploits women and children can be bought a few blocks from the White House, somebody's values have prevailed. When condoms are passed out in schools, when rap songs celebrate the murder of police, and when racism grows and festers, someone's values are prevailing. As parents we have to decide now what it is we are going to teach our children about life and death, love and sex, and freedom and slavery if we are going to insulate them from the destructive forces in modern life.

The Pulitzer-Prize-winning and best-selling author James Michener once eloquently summed up the core values that had been taught to him by his parents when he was a child. He wrote,

> As a young man I was taught to treat all races with justice. . . . I was taught that loyalty to one's nation was an obligation. . . . I was taught the good citizen pays his taxes, supports schools, libraries and museums. I was advised to cling to good people and shun the bad, and I have tried. I realize there are considerations and pressures for young people today that did not exist for me. . . . Yet the values I learned must endure—and be taught—as the foundation for the America of tomorrow. They must be taught in the home, in religious training, in the Boy Scouts and Girl Scouts, in Little League, in the media. And most critically, as a guarantee that everyone will be exposed to them, they must be taught in school.

These are wise words from a great man. Michener believed that "the home still ought to be the cradle of all values."[1] Michener knew that parents are the first and most important teachers a child has.

I want to share with you what we are teaching our children in our home. It is my hope that millions of other children will be taught the same, not because they are the values of the Bauer family, but because they are the lessons of the good life that the long history of civilization and trial and error have taught us. If we will teach these first principles to all of our children, regardless of race or economic background, I am convinced we will take a major step on our journey home to a good and decent society.

1. The most important thing we can teach our children is that each human being is a unique creature of God. From the earliest possible moment we have tried to teach our children this simple fact. Everything else we hope to teach them ultimately rests upon this basic truth. I believe the knowledge that there is a loving Father who created them and loves them and cares about them *individually* is the key to Elyse, Sarah, and Zachary getting through the inevitable defeats and disappointments they will encounter in life. We have found that the only way to teach this lesson is to make sure that God is part of their everyday lives as a family. Grace before meals, church attendance, and studying Scripture together are all important activities that can bring your family together and prepare your children to face and reject the temptations they will certainly encounter.

2. Second, we have tried to teach our children that the most important things can't be bought. The materialism of modern life is everywhere. Children, particularly, are deeply influenced by the rampant commercialism in our society that places a price tag on everything. In the inner cities children are sometimes murdered for a pair of Reeboks or a leather jacket. In the upscale suburbs too many parents try to substitute cars, top-of-the-line vacations, or cold, hard cash for the time and love their children need the most.

While driving through Washington, D.C. recently, I spotted a sports car ahead of me with a bumper sticker that read, "The One Who Dies with the Most Toys Wins." I don't know if the driver was trying to be ironic or not. In any case the bumper sticker represents an empty and failed philosophy of life. What a contrast to the needlepoint I once saw hanging in a kitchen that said, "It is better to live rich than to die rich." My good friend, nationally known investment counselor Ronald Blue, often reminds his audiences of successful businessmen that no one has ever seen a funeral hearse pulling a U-Haul behind it. His point: We come into the world without any possessions, and we will leave it the same way.

A few years ago our children were disappointed that we couldn't afford to take the same kind of "upscale" vacation as some of our more affluent neighbors. It was a good opportunity to remind them of the circumstances surrounding my own childhood. I grew up in a reasonably happy, blue-collar family, but money was always a problem. My father had dropped out of high school to help his parents through the Depression years. His lack of education and training kept him in low-paying, unskilled jobs all his life. I often watched my parents sit at the kitchen table on

Friday night, payday, and with furrowed brows carefully divide Dad's salary into several stacks for bills.

To this day I don't know how my mother was able to manage our resources from week to week with so little money at her disposal. But she did, and I love and respect her for it. But even her efforts couldn't produce money when there was little.

There was seldom anything left over for savings and certainly nothing for frivolous expenditures. In all my years of living at home, we were never able to go away on a vacation, nor did we ever own a new car. (In fact, the history of the Bauer automobile "lemons" would be a book in itself.) I never flew on a plane, saw the ocean, or had more than one suit (usually worn only on Sunday morning). Yet we were fortunate compared to families just a few blocks away in the west end of the city, across the proverbial railroad tracks. Many of them would have given anything to be as financially "secure" as we were.

Sometimes not having more money was painful and frustrating. The taunts of children from "better" families still ring in my ears. But looking back on it now, the lack of financial resources actually provided an opportunity for me at a young age to build character and understand the value of a dollar. Many children today are desperately poor, and that is a national tragedy which must be addressed. But other children may end up poor in a more profound and lasting way if they become convinced that money is the key to their happiness and success in life.

There are many things we can do in our own homes to help our children gain perspective on wealth and possessions. We put money in its proper place by being generous in sharing our good fortune with those in need. And, in fact, millions of other Americans are doing the same. Recent studies show that giving and charitable work are at all-time highs.

Teach your children to give of their talents and treasure. One of the many negative consequences of our current welfare system is that it provides an excuse for us to feel that the poor are being taken care of by government and that we have no personal individual obligation to do anything else to help. That is a tragedy. The great secret of giving is what it does not only for the one in need, but for the giver too. No institutionalized bureaucracy can accomplish as much as individual men and women working together.

Each of our children must be taught that they have a personal responsibility to help those less fortunate than themselves. Every year our children have been encouraged to go through their toys and select some to give to the needy kids program run by the United States Marine Corps in the Washington, D.C. area. We urge our children to give a portion of their allowances and earnings from odd jobs to the church for special missions and aid to the poor.

Here, too, nothing teaches as powerfully as example. Carol and I have made it a particular priority to help crisis pregnancy centers around the country that provide food, housing, and moral encouragement to young women who reject abortion and give birth to an "unplanned" child. Last Christmas we helped an organization provide gifts to children whose parents were dying from AIDS.

We believe it is also important to help our children gain an appreciation of the things in life that are available to all of us by God's mercy *without cost.* Sharing a beautiful sunset or standing outside together on a clear night to look into the starry skies overhead cannot only create memories but also help children to gain a sense of perspective.

On most days I get up, drive to work, and spend the day fighting for family values in Washington, D.C. My life revolves around court cases, congressional hearings, press interviews, and meetings at the White House. I believe it is important work, and I am thankful for the opportunity to influence public policy and to fight for the values I believe most Americans are still committed to. Like most of you, I work hard and take my work seriously.

Occasionally, however, I find myself in different surroundings. In recent years my family and I have spent a few days each fall at a ranch in Montana, far from the wars in Washington. Getting to Elk Canyon isn't easy. We usually travel all day, often have to deal with canceled or late flights because of bad weather, and generally have to put up with all of the frustrations that go with long family trips. (Most of them summed up by five little words: "Dad, are we there yet?")

Finally, late into the night, we're on the last leg of the trip, a long drive through the dark landscape of Montana. Through the window I can see the brilliant stars that are visible in Big Sky country but are hidden by the bright lights of Washington, D.C. In the rearview mirror my wife and I can see our three children, serenely asleep and dreaming future dreams.

Hundreds of years ago pioneer families braved the elements and many more dangers than we did to make this same trip, searching for a place to settle down and raise their children. The years pass, but the patterns are the same.

There is a permanency about family life and about faith that transcends anything that may happen in Washington, D.C. On those long drives in Montana I am often reminded once again of those permanent things of hearth and home. The troubles of the day are put in their rightful perspective.

We are never too old to relearn this lesson. I recently shared with an associate my worry and consternation over the loss of value in my home. Like most Americans our house is our largest asset, or at least it was. I have been banking on it to help send our children to college. But recently we discovered that a massive underground oil spill from a nearby tank farm is steadily moving toward our neighborhood. I have watched helplessly as our property's value plummets. My friend sympathized with my plight, but then he helped put my concerns in perspective. "Gary, we are constantly being taught that there is no security in things—not property, or IRA's, or insurance policies. In the final analysis we have to rely on faith."

3. Our children must be taught that we unconditionally love them. One of the great tragedies of our times is that so many of our children feel unloved and in many cases are unloved. The most obvious examples shout at us in each morning's headlines—abused children, abandoned children—children without hope.

Alex Kitlowitz in his stunning book, *There Are No Children Here,* paints a picture of the despair that grips too many of our inner-city children who have been abandoned by their fathers and are surrounded by drugs, violence, and poverty. But in the fashionable suburbs, too, there are children who have been abandoned and are unloved. Children must have an adult in their life who makes them their most important priority before a job, before the possibility of a new spouse, before anything else. It is a tragedy when there is just one child for whom there is no such adult. Today there are millions of such children.

We can show our love for our kids in a thousand ways, but the simplest way of all is to clearly tell them, time and time again. When our own children are facing a challenge, Carol and I are quick to remind them that no matter how things come out, we love them. They are loved if they bring home A's or D's. They are loved if they do well at sports or if they follow their father's less sterling athletic record. They are loved if they win a school election or if they come in last. I don't believe children instinctively know this. In our success-oriented society many kids feel parental love is conditioned on performance. It shouldn't be and we should remind them it isn't.

Don't ignore or forget the little things—a hug, a note in a lunch box, a smile, a nighttime kiss. Children thrive on these simple acts of caring. It is these things that will be remembered not only during a bad day, but long after your time with them is gone.

4. Children must be taught that choices have consequences. Choice has become a highly esteemed American value in recent years. Public figures often talk about it as if it were an end in itself. Of course, in reality it is not merely choice but *what* we choose that is the most important thing. Some choices are better, more sound than others. Our children must be taught this basic fact.

Choices do have consequences. The child who opts for television instead of studying the night before an exam will suffer the consequence of a low grade. Too much of today's educational enterprise is focused on helping children think about choices instead of focusing on what the right choices are. Research shows that children want guidance and direction. Show your children what experience has taught you about the choices they face today. Point them in the right direction. Explain to them that, as the children of free men and women, they do have rights, but they also have responsibilities.

Rights vs. Duties

While our popular culture, from Hollywood to Washington, emphasizes rights, I believe Americans, including our children, are hungry for a new sense of duty and responsibility. The Russian dissident Aleksandr Solzhenitsyn looked at American society and concluded, "There has been a sweeping away of duties and an expansion of rights. But we have two lungs. You can't breathe with just one lung and not with the other. We must avail ourselves of rights and duties in equal measure."

Our republic was built on the idea that each of us would limit our own behavior even if the law did not require it. Most Americans practice such restraint and are anxious for the culture to reinforce their choices. Children, particularly, need that reinforcement.

5. Each child should be given reliable standards of right and wrong. Our culture is permeated with the philosophy of relativism. All of us receive constant messages that we must be nonjudgmental. We are told that what is right for one person could be wrong for another. Allan Bloom in his book, *The Closing of the American Mind,* says that the freshman students at the University of Chicago where he teaches come from diverse social, racial, and economic backgrounds. But they are the same in one important respect. Almost all of them reject the idea of universal standards of right and wrong. No wonder our society is overwhelmed with street criminals, ripoff artists, tax cheaters, savings-and-loan embezzlers, and corrupt politicians. Moral relativity has no socioeconomic bounds!

The conservative writer and philosopher Russell Kirk has observed, "What gives a man dignity, and what makes possible a democracy of elevation, and what makes any society tolerable, and what gives just leaders their right to office, and what keeps the modern world from being a Brave New World and what constitutes real success in any walk of life, is private moral worth." Thomas Jefferson told his nephew to pursue his own interests and that of his country with the "purest integrity, the most chaste honor. . . . Give up money, give up fame, give up science, give up the earth itself and all it contains rather than do an immoral act. And never suppose that in any possible situation or under any circumstances that it is best for you to do a dishonorable thing, however slightly so it may appear to you." This is the kind of advice our children need now. They may not hear it in the classroom, though they should. The popular culture certainly won't teach it to them. They need to hear it from us early and often.

There are many ways to pass on these standards without merely lecturing. There is a rich cultural history of facts and myth that can help us pass on to our children the moral compass they need. The most obvious place, of course, is our religious heritage. To really get back to basics start with the Decalog or Ten Commandments. In these clear rules of living we have been given more wisdom than countless lawyers and law books have been able to produce.

The noted host of ABC's popular "Nightline," Ted Koppel, told a Duke University graduating class a few years ago that, "What Moses brought down from Mount Sinai were not the Ten Suggestions. They are commandments. Are, not were. The sheer brilliance of the Ten Commandments is that they codify in a handful of words acceptable human behavior, not just for then or now, but for all time." Though I may not agree with Ted Koppel on everything, on this point we are of like mind.

We must expose our children to lofty ideas and uplifting concepts. As Paul wrote, "Whatever things are true, whatever things are noble, whatever things are just, whatever things are pure, whatever things are lovely, whatever things are of good report, if there is any virtue and if there is anything praiseworthy—meditate on these things." As parents we know that if much is expected of our children, much will be accomplished. And the reverse is true too. If, by our words and actions, it is clear we expect little of them by not challenging them intellectually and spiritually, their growth will be stunted.

Our history and literature are rich with stories to help our children understand reliable standards of right and wrong. I grew up in schools that taught us stories like that of George Washington and the cherry tree to transmit the value of truthfulness. Sadly today many of these stories have been dropped from textbooks and replaced with politically correct substitutes that teach nothing about life or our heritage.

One of the undiscovered attractions in Washington, D.C. is Theodore Roosevelt Island, an eighty-eight-acre wilderness preserve located in the Potomac River. There, on the northern center of the island is a formal memorial, a seventeen-foot bronze statue of the former President. The statue overlooks an oval terrace from which rise four twenty-one-foot granite tablets, each inscribed with the Roosevelt philosophy of citizenship.

The tablet titled "Youth" has these memorable words: "I want to see you game, boys [and girls may I add]. I want to see you brave and manly, and I also want to see you gentle and tender. Be practical as well as generous in your ideals. Keep your eyes on the stars, but remember to keep your feet on the ground. Courage, hard work, self-mastery, and intelligent effort are all essential to successful life. Alike for the Nation and the individual, the one indispensable requisite is character."

In the final analysis, though, the best way we can teach reliable standards of right and wrong as well as character is through the examples of our own lives. You can't teach a child honesty if he sees you cutting corners in your own life. You can't teach loyalty if you fail to keep your own commitments to your spouse, community, church, or friends.

Dennis Rainey, in his book *Pulling Weeds, Planting Seeds,* writes of how the example of his father influenced his own life. He says that his father "did what was right, even when no one was looking. I never heard him talk about cheating on taxes. . . . His integrity was impeccable. I never heard him lie, and his eyes always demanded the same truth in return." We could accomplish nothing in our lives more important than to have our children someday be able to say the same of each of us.

6. We need to give them the character to stand against the crowd. Our children are under incredible peer pressure in our trend-conscious world. They get countless messages telling them what they should wear, what they should listen to and what they should do with their bodies. Following the crowd on minor things, of course, usually doesn't matter in the long run, but following the crowd on sex, drugs, or violence can have a profound impact on the type of adults our children grow up to be or whether, in this dangerous world, they are fortunate enough to grow up at all.

Peer pressure is an awesome force. It may be funny when such pressure results in an almost overnight shift in acceptable teenage clothes, music, or slang. But the process of losing our individuality to the crowd is no laughing matter. Mobs are composed not merely of evil men but of average people caught up in the excitement of the moment. I once read a fascinating and chilling study of German soldiers during World War II who were responsible for executing hundreds and sometimes thousands of Jewish prisoners at a time. The researchers found that even near the end of the war, when some "lax" commanders allowed the soldiers to "opt out," many of them continued to perform their deadly assignment. Studies show that many of these murderers were not hardened SS troops. Rather, they were average men, most of them nonideological shopkeepers and factory workers conscripted into the German army. In interviews after the war they told shocked investigators that they proceeded with the executions out of fear of being ridiculed by their peers! Peer pressure led them to barbarism.

Our children must be taught to have the courage to stand apart from the crowd. Sometimes the best way to teach that lesson is by us as parents being willing to say no. Every parent has heard the protest, "But everyone is doing, seeing, buying, going to it." Our response has always been, "But we aren't everybody's parents—we are yours. You're not everyone—you are our daughter." These episodes are never easy, but the long-term reward for standing firm will be great. And even in the short-term you can sometimes see the payoff.

A few years ago when our older daughter was in the sixth grade, she was invited to what has become a suburban tradition, a Friday night sleepover. Once there she discovered that one of the movies that had been rented that night was rated PG-13, a movie we had previously told her was off-limits. It would have been relatively easy for her to watch the movie without her mother and me finding out. Instead she called home and told us the situation. Her girlfriends wouldn't give in on the choice of the movie, so we picked Elyse up early that night before it was shown. It was a tough situation for her to endure at a time when the last thing a pre-teen wants to do is to stand out from the crowd. But ultimately it cost her no real friends.

As Elyse has matured into a young lady, the character she demonstrated that night has grown stronger. In high school today she is seen as a principled young lady with high standards who is willing to stand up for what she believes. She was even elected senator of her freshman class. Kids are influenced by peer pressure, but they are also looking for leadership!

7. Every child must understand the sacredness of human life. One of the most disturbing trends in our society is the growing tendency to see some lives as being more valuable than others. Coupled with this is a growing disrespect for life in general. Our cities increasingly are the scenes of murderous violence committed for no apparent reason other than to impress or to establish a reputation. A crime of passion can at least be explained. But how can we make sense of the random killings that seem to occur with more and more frequency?

The sacredness of life is under attack in other ways. Medical breakthroughs enable us to increasingly play God with life in the womb. Prenatal tests that may show deformity now routinely result in abortion. I wonder if we realize what we are losing in the process of "weeding out" those unborn children who are not physically perfect.

I had the honor recently to give an award to a courageous woman by the name of Judy Squier. Judy by anyone's definition would be considered a winner. She has a happy marriage and is raising three well-adjusted children. She is active in her church and in community affairs in her hometown in California. A lot of people can boast of having these same accomplishments, of course, but what makes Judy extraordinary is that she has done all this even though she was born with no legs. After her birth a heartless obstetrician left the delivery room and informed her waiting father, "Your daughter is going to live, I'm sorry to say." That medical professional was very aware of Judy's obvious outward deformities. But with all his knowledge of the human body he had no way to take the measurement of character, her heart and soul. In those areas Judy benefited from a surplus.

With the guidance of her father and the support of her family, Judy's life has turned the obstetrician's observation into a lie. Early on she resolved herself to working harder and longer than "normal" people for what she wanted. Her life was a series of setbacks followed by eventual triumphs. Today she drives a specially designed car and is a regular Mom to her children and wife to her husband.

When Judy was in Washington she had an opportunity to talk to many members of the U.S. Senate, all of whom praised her for the example she has set. Judy was grateful for the praise and adulation. But she shocked the senators, many of whom described themselves as pro-choice, when she remarked that if they had their way there would be no Judy Squiers in the future. Abortion would eliminate the "deformed" and "abnormal" children like herself long before they had a chance to see the light of the world and long before we could experience the light of their lives.

Judy told the audience the night she received her award, "I am convinced that this old world needs handicapped people. God designed it that way. Handicapped people make a unique contribution that cannot be synthesized." There wasn't one person in the audience, most of them in tears, who would disagree.

Congressman Henry Hyde, a great friend and public servant, once asked me if I had ever thought of a time in history or a historical event that I would have liked to witness firsthand? He personally chose the Vienna Opera House on May 7, 1824. It was on that evening that Beethoven, for the first time, directed the premiere performance of his moving Ninth Symphony. When he was finished, the members of the orchestra rushed to his side and turned him around to face the audience so he could see their reaction, the thunderous applause, and the tears. They did this because Beethoven was completely deaf. He could not hear one note of the symphony that he just conducted. Some people believe that symphony is the most divinely inspired piece of music ever created.

One doesn't have to search for a Beethoven to find that unique spark that exists in each human being. Henry Hyde has also written and spoken about Greg Wittine, who became an Eagle Scout when he was twenty-three years old. Hyde in his excellent book, *For Every Idle Silence,* says this of Wittine:

> Cerebral paralytic. Sits in a wheelchair. Can't talk. You'd think he was retarded; has little control over his musculature; points to the letters of an alphabet to communicate. I watched him on television become an Eagle Scout. His chest was covered with merit badges. On the best day I ever lived, I couldn't have earned 10 percent of those merit badges. Hike ten miles? He crawled one mile and then pushed his wheelchair the other nine.
>
> If you deny the existence of the human soul, then you have a responsibility to define the celestial fire in Greg Wittine who says: "I won't surrender to my handicaps. I'm going to achieve. I'm going to do the best I can with what God has given me."[2]

Our children need to know of such people. They also must be taught that the measure of a man or woman is not found in the shape or form of their body, nor in the outward quality of their life. In each of us there is a celestial fire, a divine spark that marks us as a special creation of God.

8. Children need to know that through hard work they can overcome almost anything. The American dream has taken a lot of knocks lately, but I believe it is still alive and well. Our nation was founded on the notion that all the citizens of a free society could go as far as their talents and hard work would take them. Today many children, often reflecting the views of the adults around them, believe that the "deck is stacked" and that hard work is for suckers. What a tragedy! The implications for our future are sobering.

Research shows that a major factor in the success of recent immigrants—particularly the Vietnamese—is that they have been taught the elements of the American dream: hard work, effort, excellence, responsibility. When I was under secretary of education and I spoke of this fact to an audience of public school officials, one skeptic stood up and said, "Well, that's very interesting but those are 'oriental' values and not particularly relevant to American children." Oriental values? Yes, there are eastern cultures that embrace these ideas, but not just those cultures. Had my questioner never heard of Ben Franklin, the Protestant work ethic, McGuffey's readers? These values informed us during the years of our most vibrant growth and expansion. We must reinstill them now in our children if our nation is going to be competitive again.

9. All of our children, black and white must be taught to reject the insidious virus of racism. "F'eedom." The little girl's pronunciation of the word is one of the most evocative moments in Martin Luther King's writings. It was her answer to a question about the meaning of the civil rights movement. Like the salute of the little boy as the caisson passed carrying the body of his father, the slain president, it spoke more eloquently than the orations of many grownups who witnessed the same events.

When the city of Los Angeles erupted just after Easter 1992, and more people were killed and more damage was done than in any urban rioting in modern U.S. history, the eloquence of children became obvious once again. Several days after the riots began with the acquittal of four police officers in the beating of Rodney King, a terrible, less-noticed tragedy occurred just a few miles from where we live. Joseph A. Ford was a thirteen-year-old honor student who lived in Prince George's County, a suburb of Washington, D.C. Joey spoke at the Three Way Deliverance Church on the Friday evening after the riots. He talked about violence and drugs and urged the black congregation to remember that the answer to these problems and all others was salvation through Christ. Moments later, while Joey and his family drove home, he was killed by a single bullet fired in the middle of a shootout between rival drug pushers.

Joey's tragic death received a little local coverage, but few politicians dwelled on it and few words of outrage were heard. Such deaths in our inner cities at the hands of thugs are all too common.

The real division in our nation is not between black and white. Rather on one side are good people, like Joey, who believe in reliable standards of right and wrong, the golden rule, faith, and family. And on the other side are those who reject these values and all that they stand for.

Amidst all the smoke and fire, the fear and hopelessness, more than a few candles of courage were brightly lit. In the first few terrifying hours of violence in south central Los Angeles, several people who happened to be in the wrong place at the wrong time were pulled from their vehicles and brutally beaten. Television cameras caught much of the violence as it happened and broadcast it live. It sickened all of us. While an angry mob roamed the streets, at least four residents of the city who lived nearby were moved to help. They rushed to the scene and intervened to rescue a truck driver who had been pulled from his cab and surrounded by attackers.

Two of the four were interviewed shortly after by NBC's Tom Brokaw. He asked one of them, actor Gregory Alan-Williams, how he found it in himself to risk his own life, to do something so selfless as to come to the aid of a total stranger. The answer was riveting:

> You see, some people have said it was a selfless act, but on my part it was a very selfish act, and the reason is because as I stood there and watched them beating him, my thought was, "If I don't help this man, when and if the mob comes for me, there'll be nobody there to help me." Dr. King said, "We're tied in a single garment of destiny, and whatever affects one directly affects all of us indirectly."[3]

When our children see the headlines about death and destruction, parents must make certain they also learn of the stories like these. First, because they may not make the headlines, the quiet, daily courage of the citizens who struggle to make something out of south central Los Angeles or the south Bronx is almost never in the news. Second, because this is the way healing begins, in the very same moment that the wounding occurs.

Days after the riot, Academy Award-winning actor Lou Gossett, Jr. delivered a commencement speech at the New England Institute of Technology in Providence. He told the graduates that the antidote to violence is family. "I can't emphasize enough," he told the students, who greeted him with a standing ovation, "the need for you young people to take your knowledge, your heart, and your energy out into the mainstream of this country with a very strong sense of family."

Gossett told the graduates of his own life growing up in a melting-pot neighborhood in south Brooklyn. There he never encountered the meaning of race or class divisions. But when he was a teenager in the 1950s, he took a train trip to Georgia to visit relatives. Just south of the Mason-Dixon line, in Baltimore, he was forced to get aboard a segregated train to complete his journey. But, he said, by this stage of his life his family had nurtured him so well that he never doubted himself. "It never occurs to me," he said, "that I'm different from anyone else."[4]

Gossett made his career break in the television series made from Alex Haley's *Roots.* After Haley's recent death, *Washington Post* reporter Juan Williams wrote how Haley's latest project, left uncompleted, had been an effort to demonstrate the absurdity of racial divisions in a world composed not of two colors, but many shades. It had grieved him to see how far we remained from a world that judged by the content of the character, not the color of the skin.

I grew up in the era of segregation in a state where there was plenty of feeling on both sides and a lot in between. The family house in Newport is just blocks from the Ohio River. Across the river is Cincinnati, which saw its own scaled-down version of the long, hot summer of '65, the riots that gripped the nation from Watts to the Motor City to Washington, D.C.

Some philosophers and writers have argued that family is the enemy of brotherhood. That the narrow interests of one's clan or upbringing stand in the way of identification with the larger community or the cosmos. As you can guess, I'm not one of them.

Lou Gossett is right. Family and a community of families are the best place for the unlearning of bigotry, the begetting of tolerance. Every child with siblings and other children as neighbors must learn early of the meaning of compromise and sharing. Today you can walk through a massive toy emporium like Toys 'R Us and forget the world wasn't always like that. When I was little, you could tell how old a buddy's bike was by how many layers of paint were on it, sort of like the rings on a tree.

New bikes were rare. If someone had one, you figured his Dad had just gotten a promotion or bowled 230 in the Wednesday night league and bought it in a moment of delirium. If you were really unlucky, you inherited your sister's bike, with the easy step-over bar. Other kids on the block said things. Your skin got pretty thick after awhile.

Like most adults, I don't remember when, as a child, I first really noticed that, thick or thin, human skin came in different shades. I believe someone must have told me. I know that my own children didn't really notice until someone, a playmate or an adult, said something to them that didn't make much sense unless there was a difference there that they were supposed to see.

Growing up I noticed differences of poverty before I noticed any of race. The Cincinnati area had its share of both poor whites and blacks, Appalachian people and families moved up from the South during the Civil War and the later migrations to the industrial North.

My father would take me to baseball games at old Crosley Field, home of the Redlegs. The old park, with its red-and-white paint and brocade of painted wood over the facade of the stands (it always reminded me of the painted wood on the steamboats that plied the river), stood just north of the city's west end. It was a poor neighborhood, and on hot summer nights before the ball games, street vendors would stand on the corners selling discount bags of peanuts out of big cardboard boxes. The old men of the neighborhood, whom I remember as always looking thin, sat on the stoops of the brick row houses and watched the crowd moving up the street.

Once inside the ballpark, all my heroes were on an equal footing—Jim O'Toole, Frank Robinson, Gene Freese, Vada Pinson. An equal footing way beyond my plane. But the outside world *was* different. It was headed toward explosions I only dimly understood. But I did understand give and take. My family had been a shield from the damage that prejudice and hatred could do. Years later, I read Martin Luther King's "Letters from the Birmingham Jail." I understood better than ever that an equal footing wasn't just a playing field for heroes, but the natural right of everybody in the game.

It would be better if we could all unlearn the moments when we first "noticed." Or forget the first slur spoken around us or written on a boarded-up window. It would be better still if those windows were opened up, the painted flowers and sills taken down, and the streets and houses filled again with families. We're riding the same train now.

It's not exactly bedtime reading, but our children must know about letters written from jail cells. The times demand it. If they do, a time will come when our whole nation will sleep easier at night, as we should, like babies in the common cradle of our humanity.

10. Our children must be taught a rational love of their country and the essence of the requirements of citizenship. My father served in World War II. He saw battle in the South Pacific, was wounded, and received decorations. He came home after the war and began his life again. I was born the year after the war ended. He stayed married to the same wife for forty-nine years and raised a family in a small city on the Ohio River. When he was older and became sick, he went for treatment to the Veterans Hospital in Cincinnati. He died in 1990.

My father served this country, and never for a moment did he regret it. But he shook his head a great many times before he died, wondering what had become of the things for which he and so many members of his generation had fought. He was an extraordinary man. Even though there were millions like him. They were an extraordinary generation that made extraordinary sacrifices. But they were ordinary Americans.

When the Berlin Wall fell and Soviet communism collapsed, it was a victory not only for freedom but for families. Families that laid, to paraphrase Lincoln, so many costly sacrifices on freedom's altar.

That is not to engage in jingoism or an excessive pride in ourselves. It was the Roman Empire's practice to demand tribute of conquered nations, to be paid to the emperor's coffers in exchange for the return of captured family members. If America has an empire, it is an odd one. Our tributes have been paid out in blood and repaid only in a new kinship with those nations against whose governments we fought.

This struck me anew when I read the recent words of Manfred Rommel, mayor of Stuttgart and the son of the Desert Fox, the crafty German Field Marshal, Erwin Rommel, who became disillusioned with Hitler and took his own life as an alternative to trial over his alleged involvement in an assassination plot against the Führer. As the U.S. Seventh Corps left Stuttgart, part of the winding down of the U.S. presence in Europe, Mayor Rommel stood and told these Americans, "I want to express my gratitude to the United States and to the U.S. Army for forty-seven years of peace."

Forty-seven years of peace in Europe—that is what the families of my father's generation sacrificed for. That is why today's dividends of peace properly belong to families, to the sons and daughters they came home to raise. Those children, exemplified by the men and women of the Seventh Corps, have served, too, for family and freedom. And we must never forget, nor allow our children to forget, what our forefathers brought forth anew just two score and seven years ago.

Our children must know their story. Not just the story of the veterans of World War II and the conflicts since, but of those who fought and died at Concord and Shiloh, at San Juan Hill and Belleau Wood. They must know why the French changed the name of Belleau Wood to Bois de la Brigade de Marine in honor of the Americans who fought there. They must know the width of the shoulders on which they stand. They must see the honor rolls. They must know that war, even when just, is always a tragedy. But they must also know that they live in a nation which fought its wars against the greater tragedies of tyranny and injustice. A nation whose only occupied foreign territory, as President Reagan said on the fortieth anniversary of the invasion of Normandy, is the burial ground in which our fallen heroes lie.

Our children must also know about the architects of their liberty. Not merely those who wielded the pen of the Declaration and the Constitution, but those who shaped railroad ties, bent their necks before the blast furnaces, riveted the girders into place, watched over the childish brows hot with scarlet fever, built and tended the clapboard-covered houses and the picket-fenced yards. America did not spring up as water from the desert, it was dredged up from thorn and thistle by the labor of many generations.

President Reagan once received a moving letter from a U.S. sailor stationed on the carrier *Midway,* which was then patrolling the South China Sea. It was during the early eighties and the horrible exodus of "boat people" from Vietnam was at its peak. The sea was teeming with boats filled with desperate people, most having literally nothing left in their possession other than the shirts on their backs. Many died during the trip, but they braved the seas rather than live under an oppressive communist regime.

The sailor scanned the horizon and spotted one of the craft, a leaky little boat with refugees crammed inside. The skipper of the *Midway* sent out a launch to rescue them. As the wet and cold families were brought to the ship, one of the refugees spotted the sailor on deck. He stood up, and with all the strength he had left after a journey we can't possibly imagine, he yelled, "Hello American sailor. Hello, freedom man!"

President Reagan loved this story. He never tired of telling it to us in White House lunch meetings or using it in his speeches when he urged Americans to remember their heritage. I think the president liked the story because it reminded him of another "freedom man," John Winthrop, an early Pilgrim who, when he arrived, described the new nation as a "shining city upon a hill." In Reagan's farewell address, he described what he thought that shining city was all about. He said,

> In my mind it was a tall proud city built on rocks stronger than oceans, wind swept, God blessed, and teeming with people of all kinds living in harmony and peace, a city with free ports that hummed with commerce and creativity, and if there had to be city walls, the walls had doors and the doors were open to anyone with the will and the heart to get here. That's how I saw it, and see it still.

And that's who we are at our best. A nation of families, different in countless ways, but alike in our fundamental commitment to ordered liberty under God. We are Irish cab drivers and

Italian cops. We are Korean shopkeepers and Mexican day laborers. We are Black teachers and German mill workers. All of us "freedom men" and women, family men and women.

America is the town hall. The Lions Club and the volunteer fire department. It is the DAR and the PTA. Babe Ruth baseball and Pop Warner football. The Chinese-American Friendship League and the Sons of Italy. It is the place of *Future Shock* and of *Roots.* It is 3.6 million square miles with scarcely a corner of its vast reach unetched with history. It is a place always inclined to think of itself as young and new. But, as one glance at the red brick and rust of the great cities of the Midwest and Northeast will tell you, it has been around a long while. The blood of many families is in those bricks, the residue of much sweat and tears in that rust. These are the shoulders upon which our children sit. They must not forget. This is home.

7

The Literature of Family, Faith, and Freedom

OF ALL THE LITTLE RITUALS that are part of day-to-day family life, the bedtime story may be the most delightful. In many homes, ours included, those important moments alone with your children at the end of a long day can be the most satisfying moments you spend.

Magic can take place in a rocking chair in a child's bedroom. Our history can be brought to life. Values can be passed on. Your son or daughter may realize for the first time that the symbols on a page mean something. In those quiet moments the groundwork is laid for children to develop their own love of reading and of learning.

The real value of reading to our children can't be captured by research studies or statistics. Frozen in my mind are the expressions of wonderment on my children's faces when they were first introduced to the power of stories. Reading to your children the "Midnight Ride of Paul Revere" or some other adventure poem or story is an exercise in watching imagination come alive. Little eyes grow bigger. Young faces brighten with wonder and excitement. Those minutes in the evening before bedtime when the house grows quiet and there is an opportunity to read to my children have become one of the most looked-forward-to activities of the day.

Of course now both of my daughters read on their own. Sarah not only loves reading, but her fascination with words and expressions has turned her into an aspiring writer. This summer she has actually been accepted into a special course at a local university for writers. Elyse spends hours with books. Zachary tends to be more physical and would prefer to wrestle with me than sit still long enough to read a book. But Carol, with her patience, is able to get him to sit still long enough for some good bedtime stories.

Reading is a great way, before prayers, to prepare a child for bedtime. I must confess though that more than once over the years I have taken one of the kids up to their room to read in the hopes it would help put them to sleep, only to drop off myself in the rocking chair after an exhausting day.

When I was very young, my grandmother spent hours reading to me. I was fascinated by the childhood stories she shared and the little asides she would add to make those stories even more vivid and alive. After my grandmother's death, my mother did most of the reading. My father preferred to sit at the side of my bed in the evening and tell me stories he knew by memory. Together, all of them instilled in me a love for books. And that love of books helped me to overcome the odds and get through college and law school.

The love of reading often comes long before the reading itself is possible. Each of our children went through the stage of sitting with a book in their hands (sometimes upside down) and repeating a story from memory as if they were reading it.

Best Kept Secrets

At the earliest ages children must depend on us if they are going to develop a love of reading. First Lady Barbara Bush has called reading aloud to your children "one of the best-kept secrets of good parenting. . . . Reading teaches sharing and involvement. It brings families together and makes children feel loved."

She is right. In my work at the Department of Education we discovered that reading aloud to young children can give them a two-and-a-half-year head start in reading readiness by the time they begin school. Mrs. Bush urges parents to take seven steps to make reading part of their family life: "(1) Get started now (don't procrastinate); (2) Make reading aloud a habit; (3) Involve the whole family; (4) Keep books handy; (5) Choose good books; (6) Make the written word come alive (by involving the child in the story); and (7) Keep reading to them after they can read for themselves."[1]

The question of what you should read to your children is just as important as getting them into the habit of reading. We have found that even at the earliest ages there are stories and books available that challenge the imagination and at the same time teach values. I remember growing up with Aesop's Fables, wonderful short stories that use every child's fascination with animals to teach lessons about life.

Some of the fables are only a few paragraphs long and take only minutes to read, but each one teaches something about life and human nature. The "Wolf in Sheep's Clothing" teaches that appearances are often deceiving. "The Ant and the Grasshopper" teaches it is wise to prepare today for the wants of tomorrow. "The Goose with the Golden Eggs" explains that the greedy who want more will lose everything. "The Hare and the Tortoise" teaches us that slow and steady wins the race. "The Bundle of Sticks" teaches that there is strength in union. "The Shepherd Boy and the Wolf" teaches that liars will not be believed even when they tell the truth. Each story is short, perfect for the attention span of a young child. And because they all revolve around animals, kids are usually fascinated with the stories while learning valuable value lessons at the same time.

All of my children, when they were young, loved to have the enchanting Peter Rabbit series by Beatrix Potter read to them. Other more modern classics, like "The Little Engine That Could," can be used to teach young people the value of perseverance and trying hard until they reach their goal.

In addition to these selections, the tales of Hans Christian Anderson and the works of the Brothers Grimm all make sharp distinctions between good and evil in a context that a child's mind finds exotic and appealing. In my own childhood, I can remember my excitement when I first read Rudyard Kipling's

Jungle Book. Also by Kipling is the fascinating and moving poem "If," which is filled with wise and timely advice from a father to his son, advice from which all young children could benefit immensely. I still remember these lines:

> If you can talk with crowds and keep your virtue
> Or walk with kings—nor lose the common touch

Great advice if you're going to work in Washington, D.C. or if you find yourself in the corporate penthouse some day. The poem ends with some good advice:

> If you can fill the unforgiving minute
> With sixty seconds worth of distance run—
> Yours is the Earth and everything that's in it,
> And—which is more—you'll be a Man, my son.

Not too long ago *U.S. News & World Report* asked the American Federation of Teachers for some simple moral lessons that could be derived from children's texts. The AFT provided the example of the Bible: "And the Lord said to Cain: where is Abel, thy brother? And he said: I know not. Am I my brother's keeper? This can be used to teach responsibility. In the *Story of Pinnochio* we read, 'Lies, my dear boy, are found out immediately because they are of two sorts. There are lies that have short legs and lies that have long noses. Your lie, as it happens, is one of those that has a long nose.' This can be used to teach honesty." For older children AFT recommended *To Kill a Mockingbird* by Harper Lee. In that great book we read, "You never really understand a person until you consider things from his point of view . . . until you climb into his skin and walk around in it." This can be used to teach compassion and empathy as well as to help our children deal with racism.

What a paradox that the AFT would recommend a Bible story. Today any effort by a teacher to introduce that book into the classroom is usually greeted with outrage by the local civil libertarians on behalf of the village atheist. In fact the Supreme Court recently refused to reconsider a lower court ruling that said it was impermissible for a teacher to merely have a Bible on his desk that he read to himself during a break.

But there are many fascinating Bible stories that a child can be introduced to in the home using one of the many good children's Bibles that are on the market. All of our children were introduced at an early age to stories like David and Goliath to teach courage, Noah and the Ark to teach obedience and the ability to go against the crowd, the Good Samaritan to teach compassion for the less fortunate, and Shadrach, Meshack, and Abednego and the fiery furnace to teach faithfulness. The wonderful story of Ruth and Naomi can be used to teach family loyalty. Of course the main lesson of the Bible is the Christian story of salvation. But children can enjoy the adventure of the stories even before they are ready to deal with the idea of being reborn.

As children mature, they can be exposed to more challenging material that they can read for themselves, much of it laden with lessons about faith and home. One of my favorites is C. S. Lewis's seven-volume Chronicles of Narnia, an incredible series that will stimulate a child's imagination and entertain you as a parent, too. The first book in the series, *The Lion, the Witch, and the Wardrobe,* is the most well known, but all seven books are highly entertaining. Lewis, who had a strong Christian faith, wove the story of Christ and his victory over death throughout the Narnia series, but particularly in the first book.

He dedicated the book to his godchild, Lucy Barfield. In the paperback edition we own there is a letter in the front to her. It says:

> My dear Lucy,
>
> I wrote this story for you, but when I began it I had not realized that girls grow quicker than books. As a result you are already too old for fairy tales, and by the time it is printed and bound you will be older still. But someday you will be old enough to start reading fairy tales again. You can then take it down from some

upper shelf, dust it, and tell me what you think of it. I shall probably be too deaf to hear, and too old to understand a word you say, but I shall still be

your affectionate Godfather
C. S. Lewis[2]

Thankful parents have been taking this book down from upper shelves and dusting it off ever since, much to the delight of the children who have been introduced to the world of Narnia. I spent hours reading this classic to my daughters when they were in elementary school, and I must confess that I enjoyed it as much as they did. When they got a little older and their reading skills improved, they couldn't wait to read it themselves. Zachary is almost six now. I am looking forward to the time when he will be ready for the fascinating Narnia adventure. Don't let your children miss this wonderful series.

For high school students, Lewis's space trilogy, which is made up of three separate but continuing stories including *Out of the Silent Planet, Perelandra,* and *That Hideous Strength,* is an exciting science fiction thriller. It is also prophetic as it describes the great battle that continues to rage in the world between good and evil. Lewis himself described the series as a "fairy tale for adults."

I have great confidence in the power of stories to teach. The great Southern writer Flannery O'Connor once said that "a story is a way to say something that can't be said any other way—you tell a story because a statement would be inadequate." The literary device of showing instead of telling is a very effective way to convey truths to young minds.

There are countless other choices available that provide much more food for the mind and soul than do some of the vacuous series that are the rage among young adolescents. Books such as *The Wind in the Willows,* by Kenneth Grahame, or the great Little House on the Prairie series, by Laura Ingalls Wilder, and *The Secret Garden,* by Frances Burnett, can bring the world alive for a young child.

Susan Schaffer Macaulay, the daughter of the late Christian philosopher Francis Schaffer, has recommended a whole list of what she calls "living books." In her book *For the Children's Sake,* she urges parents to consider such wonderful selections as *Tanglewood Tales,* by Nathaniel Hawthorne; *Just So Stories,* by Rudyard Kipling; and Robert Frost's poetry. For older children there are such classics as *Jane Eyre,* by Charlotte Bronte; *Kon-Tiki,* by Thor Heyerdahl; *Oliver Twist* and *Hard Times,* by Charles Dickens; and the *Oxford Book of English Verse.*

All of these books and more are available at the fifteen thousand public libraries around the country. It doesn't take a big family income to access them but, in a world filled with other claims on a young person's time, it does take our perseverance and initiative if children are going to be exposed to good writing.

As children grow older and are exposed to more sophisticated works, they will be able to understand moral principles of a higher order. If they have been read to, they will likely have their own love of reading that will lead them to some of the great classics. Shakespeare's plays are loaded with lessons about life, virtue, and the price evil exacts. *Hamlet* is not just a morality tale which says you should not commit murder and incest; it is about the paralysis of indecision in the face of moral obligation. *King Lear* is about the ingratitude of the young, but it is also about the imperiousness of the old. Moral principles can be stated with clarity at a young age and then be refined in the higher grades. Patriotism can be presented in the first grade as a virtue, but later students should be taught that patriotism also involves being a "loving critic" when that is appropriate. "For us to love our country, our country ought to be lovely," as Edmund Burke remarked.

Our children will retain their moral principles only when they have been thoroughly explored and students have had an opportunity to see them challenged and successfully defended. Even the good people in the classics didn't always behave well. Achilles was pompous and cruel. The apostle Peter had his cowardly moments. Lancelot and Guinevere committed adultery. But these stories leave no doubt about how they should have acted, and the heavy price of their misdeeds is depicted. Children need to see that immoral actions have serious consequences, that virtue is not something you just talk about, but something you do.

Our Heritage

One of the ways we can tell our children who we are and pass on to them the values of good citizenship and character is through stories and books that transmit our heritage.

In *Fahrenheit 451,* a science fiction thriller set at some unknown time in the future, a totalitarian government strictly censors what its citizens are allowed to read. A band of rebels fights the oppressive government, but their resistance doesn't take the form of usual guerrilla movements. Instead of engaging in sabotage, murder, and mayhem, these rebels retreat to a hidden camp in the countryside. There each individual is given the responsibility of memorizing a great book so that it can be passed on to the next generation even if all copies of the book are destroyed by the government.

We are fortunate to live in a free democratic society that renounces overt censorship. Nonetheless, significant portions of our heritage are in danger of being lost out of sheer forgetfulness. The great stories of our past have slowly disappeared from textbooks. The art of reading itself is in danger as television, videos, and other forms of entertainment entice children away from books.

This is one of the areas where you as a parent can make a major difference. There are stories, books, fables, and essays that you can introduce your children to even if the local public school is not emphasizing them. From such books and stories our children can learn who they are, their heritage, and other important lessons that will serve them well throughout life.

Ronald Reagan in his farewell address to the American people on January 11, 1989, pleaded with us to teach our children the history of the nation or face the consequences.

> I'm warning of an eradication of the American memory that could result, ultimately, in an erosion of the American spirit. Let's start with some basics: more attention to American history and a greater emphasis on civic ritual. . . . And let me offer lesson number one about America: All great change in America begins at the dinner table. So tomorrow night in the kitchen I hope the talking begins.

The talking and the reading must begin. As a good first step, go to the library and find any older, general American history book. I emphasize "old" because newer books often leave out the great inspiring stories of our past. Check the index and make sure there are references to Patrick Henry, who said, "Give me liberty or give me death," and Nathan Hale, whose stirring words, "I regret I have but one life to give for my country," are included. Check to make sure that the material on our founding gives the appropriate and accurate emphasis on the role of religious belief.

Older American history books can be used to teach good character traits by using the heroic figures from our past. The story of George Washington and the cherry tree was used for years to teach children honesty. The tale of Abe Lincoln as a child walking miles to return pennies he owed makes the same point as well as teaching responsibility and making good on a debt.

We are in danger of forgetting who we are because we haven't read the "minutes of the last meeting." David McCullough, the award-winning author of numerous books including *Brave Companions,* tells a depressing story of lunching with one of Washington D.C.'s movers and shakers. He mentioned that he had spent an afternoon at Antietam:

> "What is Antietam?" she said. She is a graduate of one of our great universities. She is an editor of the op-ed page of one of our largest, most influential newspapers. . . .
>
> "Antietam," I said, "Maybe you know it as Sharpsburg." She hadn't any idea of what I was talking about.[3]

There were twenty-three thousand casualties at Antietam on September 17, 1862, the bloodiest day of our history. Our children should know of such places, what was at stake and how history was changed by the sacrifices made there. It is scandalous that an editor of an American newspaper, of all people, would not know about this great Civil War battlefield.

If our children are introduced to even a fraction of the books I have already mentioned, they will be well on their way to getting a good education. But this is not enough. All of our children need to be familiar with a core set of writings that explain who we are, our heritage as a free people, and what we believe. Some of these works can be mastered, at least at the surface level, by young children and then later understood more deeply as the child matures and is able to comprehend more.

The most important unifying values that our public schools must teach, I believe, are the fundamental principles that are the basis for our free society and democratic government.

Such documents as the Mayflower Compact, the Declaration of Independence, and the Constitution embody the values of our Western heritage. They teach such things as the inviolability of the individual, the rule of law, and the rights and duties that citizens incur when they enter into civilized society with the purpose of protecting themselves, promoting the general welfare, and enjoying freedom. The Mayflower Compact takes only a moment to read, and in that moment a child learns that "the Pilgrims came to this new land for the glory of God and advancement of the Christian faith."

In today's society, we are very conscious of "rights" whether they be civil rights or human rights. Ironically, while rights multiply in our society, we have lost our common vision of what values undergird those rights and make them worth having.

Here is my list of the central core of writing all of us should be familiar with—in no particular order. If you haven't really read some of the following, it is not too late to do so now. And if the last time you read them was to cram for a college exam, you would enjoy and benefit from rereading them now.

The Gettysburg Address

When I was growing up it was a common practice to memorize this wonderful speech, the best in our history, in honor of the fifty thousand men of the North and the South who perished at Gettysburg. All too often though, we were not always taught its full meaning and the fascinating history that surrounded the event. Today Lincoln's address at the famous Pennsylvania cemetery to honor the war dead often receives only a passing reference in school textbooks or in history classes. But in three minutes and using only 272 words, Lincoln, in the view of some scholars, arguably pulled off "a new founding of the nation."

The flawless speech is poetic and clearly displays the heavy influence of his childhood Bible reading and the effect it had on Lincoln's writings and speeches. Ironically, one part of the speech may prove to be in error. Lincoln predicts that the world would "little note nor long remember" what was said and done at Gettysburg. But we *must* remember. We should strive to make Lincoln wrong on this one count by ensuring that every educated child knows and understands what happened at Gettysburg and how America was changed by these inspired words.

The Declaration of Independence • The Constitution • The Federalist Papers

These documents are the great trilogy of the American founding. It should be impossible to graduate from an American high school without being familiar with all three. Unfortunately, even many college graduates cannot adequately discuss these works. The Federalist Papers were originally newspaper columns written by James Madison, Alexander Hamilton, and John Jay. (As George Will has pointed out, apparently the columnist profession peaked early in our history!) The columns made the essential case for our system of government with its checks and balances. William Bennett kept a tattered paperback copy of the Federalist Papers on his desk and often chose excerpts from it to teach in the many public schools he visited.

The Declaration of Independence speaks with clarity to who we are as a people and who we have been from the very beginning. "We hold these Truths to be self-evident, that all Men are created equal, that they are endowed by their Creator with certain unalienable Rights, that among these are Life, Liberty, and the Pursuit of Happiness." Think of everything your child can learn just from these words. At a time of moral relativism, the Declaration speaks of self-evident truths. It informs our children where our rights originated—with our Creator—and makes it clear that these rights cannot be taken away—they are "unalienable"—they are beyond the reach of government. The first right listed is the right to life. From it the other rights are possible, including the right to pursue happiness. American education could be mightily improved by merely reciting these words to begin each school day. Since that is unlikely to happen, you can educate your children by sharing these words with them and discussing their meaning in family conversations. There can be real "teaching moments" on holidays like July 4 when children may be particularly open to knowing more about their country.

Finally, the Constitution should be familiar to all of our children. It is the governing document of the land and the ongoing debate about its meaning is at the heart of much of our politics. You can't debate gun control, abortion, discrimination, privacy, war, or a host of other contemporary issues without knowing the framework of the discussion which our Constitution provides. Most Americans are woefully ignorant about the Constitution. I once was being interviewed by a reporter who was doing a story on school prayer. He just couldn't understand why I supported it since he said, "The Constitution says there must be a separation of church and state." When I explained to him that those words are nowhere to be found in the Constitution, he was incredulous. In fact our Constitution guarantees us the "free exercise of religion." Yet the Supreme Court in recent years seems to have forgotten the phrase. No wonder that reporter and a lot of other Americans are confused.

The Lincoln-Douglas Debates

Unfortunately, I have to spend a lot of time sitting on airplanes waiting to takeoff or land. In recent months I have filled those hours by rereading the Lincoln-Douglas debates. They represent a fascinating exercise in democracy. In the 1860s, as America lurched toward civil war, our society was deeply divided over slavery. Stephen Douglas, known as the "Little Giant," engaged in a great debate over slavery with Abraham Lincoln as they competed in the state of Illinois for a senate seat. Douglas would have been at home in today's "choice" society. It seems incredible now, but Douglas actually contended that it wasn't clear whether a black man was a person or not. Douglas believed that the most important thing was for each state to have the right to choose for itself whether it would be a free state or a slave state. Today the moral emptiness of his argument is obvious, but at the time countless Americans, North and South, to our everlasting shame, found his views compelling and persuasive.

Lincoln knew, of course, that Douglas's emphasis on choice completely ignored the moral implications of a society that would treat some men as animals. He reminded the citizens of Illinois that God had not created some men with saddles on their backs and other men with spurs on their shoes so they could ride them. Then Lincoln went to the heart of the flaw in Douglas's case: Douglas's philosophy gave choice to everyone except the person it mattered the most to—the slave. Ultimately America could not accept the moral rot we would have had to embrace if we were going to continue to tolerate slavery. We had to make a choice. Douglas believed in popular sovereignty: If the people voted for it, it was right. Lincoln believed that there were some things so heinous that the people in their collective wisdom couldn't make right even at the ballot box.

A mastery of those five pieces of our history would make any child and any parent a worthier citizen. Of course these are not the only things each of our children should read. Back in 1984 William Bennett, then chairman of the National Endowment for the Humanities, asked a host of public figures what every American should read before graduating from high school. In addition to the other writings I have already mentioned, the most popular responses were, Shakespeare (particularly *Macbeth* and *Hamlet*); Mark Twain's *Huckleberry Finn; Great Expectations* and *A Tale of Two Cities,* by Charles Dickens; the *Odyssey* and *Iliad* by Homer; Plato's *Republic; 1984* by George Orwell; *Moby Dick* by Herman Melville; John Steinbeck's *Grapes of Wrath;* Nathaniel Hawthorne's *Scarlet Letter;* Walt Whitman's *Leaves of Grass;* and Geoffrey Chaucer's *Canterbury Tales.*

All great literature has as one of its basic benefits the teaching of values. If we are going to complete our long journey home, we can begin by taking the best from literature and history to remind us of where we have been and where we want to go.

In the Schools

We know from history that all good educational systems since the time of the Roman Empire have taught the rising generation loyalty to parents and family, a sense of responsibility to the public order, a feeling of duty toward the community, a high regard for human life, respect for nature, and love of beauty and truth. A modern catalog of desired virtues that parents and teachers could agree on would be quite similar.

At a recent conference on education, Professor Christina Hoff Summers of Clark University was pressed to identify some clear issues of right and wrong by academicians who clearly felt that no such things exist. She replied:

> It is wrong to betray a friend, to mistreat a child, to humiliate someone, to torment an animal, to think only of yourself, to

> lie, to steal, to break promises. And on the positive side, it is right to be considerate and respectful of others, to be charitable, honest and forthright.

She met with a very skeptical reaction.

Of course exceptions can be found to rules such as these. The problem with modern approaches to teaching values is that they mistake the exception for the rule. A typical model problem that advocates of values clarification use on children is: What do you do if you have no money and your mother is dying of starvation? Is it all right to steal? Another common example is to ask children whom they would throw overboard if they were in a lifeboat with six people and could only stay afloat with five. These are interesting mind-bending dilemmas, but the vast majority of life's situations do not involve starving mothers and sinking lifeboats. They involve mundane things such as learning how to live in a family, showing up on time for work, displaying courtesy to fellow citizens, and discharging responsibilities to the community and country. For these tasks, fairly simple rules should suffice.

Moral education is not the same thing as religious education. Teachers in public school classrooms are not permitted to teach theology; that will have to be done in each of our homes. But constitutional prohibitions on promoting sectarian religious beliefs in our schools should not be used as an excuse to avoid teaching about the role of religion in our history and culture. Professor Paul Vitz in a Department of Education study documented a shocking bias against religion in textbooks commonly used in our schools. The Pilgrims, for example, are identified as "people who make long trips" and Christmas as "a warm time for special foods." Not only is this a form of censorship, but it severely damages our children's moral development because so many of the values Americans can agree on have as their source the Judeo-Christian ethic.

Here, for example, is a lesson from McGuffey's first reader, a very popular textbook in public schools until quite recently.

"Always do to other children as you wish them to do to you. This is the Golden Rule. So remember it when you play. Act upon it now, and when you are grown up, do not forget it." Suspicious lawyers for the American Civil Liberties Union might detect that this sounds alarmingly like something Christ once said. But what if it is? To teach about the values of the Jewish and Christian religions (as distinct from the doctrine) is to teach love, dignity, forgiveness, courage, candor, and self-sacrifice, all the highest manifestations of what it means to be alive and to be human.

The McGuffey readers were a product of William Holmes McGuffey, an outstanding nineteenth-century educator and preacher. Millions of copies were sold and widely used in American schools. Because of a renewed interest in these classic books, they are now available again through Mott Media, Inc. The seven-volume set is a treasure trove of literary selections—essays, poems, and excerpts from famous speeches by American statesmen.

Just reading the index of the fourth reader gives you a feel for the books. Included in the selections are "Washington's Birthday," "The Field of Waterloo," "The Best Classics," "Happy Consequences of American Independence," "Prince Arthur," "Anthony's Oration over Caesar," "William Tell," and dozens of other exciting writings for young people.

In our effort to identify values that can be taught in public schools, we should attempt to discover a common body of ethical knowledge that, even if it has a religious origin, serves the purpose of maintaining and strengthening devotion to our country, to democratic institutions, to fellow citizens, to family members, and finally to an ideal of human dignity.

8

Rediscovering America

To an open house in the evening
Home shall men come,
To an older place than Eden
And a taller town than Rome.

"The House of Christmas,"
Gilbert Keith Chesterton

THE LONG LINE OF CARS STRETCHING across the northern end of the Shenandoah Valley punctuates the end of a long Thanksgiving weekend. From every corner of the Midwest people are making their way back home on this Sunday night in late fall. The chain of taillights stretches across eastbound I-270 in the early evening darkness. Far ahead, like a scarlet contrail, the lights rise across the face of a mountain in the Washington Monument State Park and disappear at the summit, where the descent to D.C., Baltimore, and the other mid-Atlantic cities begins.

Washington, D.C., where my family is bound, isn't often regarded as a family city. It doesn't ordinarily appear on lists of America's most livable, or lovable, towns. But the parade of automobiles snaking across this historic valley on this traditional holiday weekend says something about even this most cynical and political of cities. A town that half-empties on Thanksgiving weekend, as cars full of parents and children struggle through the long drive to visit the folks back home, a town like that isn't entirely lost.

I admit this wasn't the thought that occurred to me the last time Carol and I made this trip. The fatigue of ten hours on the road and the crush of traffic took care of that. I wasn't thinking about the ground we were passing over either, the battlefields and history that lie all around at Sharpsburg, Hagerstown, and Gettysburg. This thought came later, as did some others.

Like the lights on those cars, America is symbolized by a certain unbroken chain of continuity. Maybe it's what Lincoln referred to as the "mystic chords of memory." Maybe it's the "green light at the end of Daisy's dock" that F. Scott Fitzgerald, who is buried up the road ahead in Rockville, described. That faraway, never quite denied, never quite attained promise of something better that motivates Americans. Maybe it's something neither past nor future, but something indelibly part of us that says, "Your mothers and fathers passed this way, in courage and hope; so must you."

Winston Churchill wrote and spoke about "the American race." What a strange way to refer to us. He could not have meant "race" in the normal sense of that word. We are a polyglot nation with every ethnic group imaginable dotting our landscape. But on further reflection perhaps it wasn't such a strange description after all. While our genetic backgrounds vary, our commitment to the idea of ordered liberty under law still unites the great majority of us. Our love of family and country, our hopes for the future, these all bind us together. In recent years we seem to have emphasized the *pluribus,* the "many," in *e pluribus unum,* but it is worth remembering not only our diversity—but also the *unum,* the things that make us one.

The traffic eases up a bit, and my foot bears down a little harder on the accelerator. Once in a while, I flick a look back at Zachary's nodding head. He is not on horseback, cradled in his mother's arms, and I am not tugging on the reins, but the glance and the worry are the same gestures of a pioneer father on the road. Sarah and Elyse doze off too, dreaming future dreams. I hold Carol's hand. Centuries have passed, but none of us are doing anything new to history. We are a family.

So several times a year we pile in the family car and go home. I still use the words, "go home," even though Carol and I have lived in Washington these many years. Our children were born here; our friends are here. For most of these friends, it is the same. There is another "home" far away from the capital.

What we call, or have called, "home" isn't so readily changed; no matter how far-flung the branches, the roots stay put. So it is with families. Pushed and pulled (punched and kicked, in some places and under some philosophies), the family stays put. In each century, it seems, one more ideology arises and vows, as a first order of business, to put the anachronism called "family" behind the human race. In its stead, this new ideology proclaims some alternative focus of human life and enterprise: the nation or the commune, the work brigade or the factory floor.

Decades later, that ideology has inevitably foundered on the rocks. But the family sails on. To paraphrase the saying, the family has buried a great many of its undertakers. And I am confident it will bury a great many more.

The desire for the familiar (literally) is family. The desire for form and commitment, duty and devotion is the family. The desire for a spouse, for children, for an ancestry and a posterity is the family. All of these things that the state can neither give nor take away. The special love that sees in another human being what is invisible to every other eye. The way a lock of hair curls. A dimple. The echo of a grandfather's gesture or a grandmother's voice in a little child. The words of wisdom and experience that are passed from one generation to another. The faith that has guided man to those shores for so many years.

Continuities that are traditions written in a language only family understands. Continuities that are part of traditions nearly all families understand. My grandfather's pocket watch. The old silver print in the hallway. The Army-issue foreign language phrase books in the old steamer trunk. A torn ticket to the Chicago World's Fair.

Not long ago, our family gathered around to watch an episode of "Brooklyn Bridge," the CBS series set in Brooklyn, New York in the '50s. The series revolves around the Berger family, immigrant Polish Jews, and the challenges they face living together during the years after World War II. Each show is an anthem to hard work, family love, faith, loyalty, and that optimism that has been so much a part of the American experience.

Tom Shales, the hard-to-please television critic of the *Washington Post,* called the show "the most savory new series of the 1992 season, the one most likely to engage the emotions, stir the heart, touch the soul—a comedy with tears that celebrates family and memory and the rich ingredients that make up the American melting pot."[1]

One of the show's most engaging characters is the maternal grandmother, Sophie Berger, who is played to perfection by actress Marion Ross. She is the lodestone of wisdom about family values who keeps her brood in line. When her eleven-year-old grandson, Alan, betrays his best friend, Benny, in order to gain the friendship of members of the neighborhood gang, she reprimands him. Sophie uses the reprimand, delivered with love, to remind her grandson of loyalty while also teaching him something about America. It is hard to capture the feeling and texture of the show by merely reading dialogue but perhaps what follows will give you a sense of its appeal, at least at our house.

Sophie: All I can say is, I am very disappointed in you, Alan. I expected more from you.

Alan: It's a little complicated, Grandma, you know.

Sophie: This is not why I came to America. No sir. This is not what I came here to find. . . .

Do you know how long I was on that boat [to America]?

I was on that boat six days. It was cold on the boat. I was hungry, I was wet. I was miserable. But one thought kept me going. One thought kept me warm at night. Gave me the courage to go on. The thought that one day I would be in America, and I would have a grandson and he would know how to be a good friend. . . .

Shame on you Alan, shame. Benny's been your best friend since you were a baby. . . . He's still your friend.

Alan: Grandma, there's a lot here I don't think you understand. There are reasons . . .

Sophie: There are always going to be reasons, Alan, to do the wrong thing. And the smarter the person is,

> the better the reasons will be. But it won't make it right. You are a smart boy, Alan. You know the difference between right and wrong. You do right, let someone else do reasons.

The show surely draws on nostalgia, but its popularity suggests the sentiments it portrays are far from dead. Millions of American families aren't tuning in because they're enchanted with some New World version of "the olde curiosity shoppe." No, they must see in "Brooklyn Bridge" something like themselves, or something they would like to think about themselves. About their country. About the special pulling together that family is.

The show also says a lot about the strong women who have been such a part of American life long before shrill feminism came on the scene. Marion Ross has talked about how she has fleshed out the role of Sophie Berger.

> I come from these Irish ancestors, and this kind of strength in a woman is not uncommon to the women *who were everywhere* when I was growing up. There was an era when women lived for families; there were immigrants who lived for the next generation—women stop me on the street and say they identify with that approach to life. Now every grandmother is out doing their thing, getting divorced, getting her hair done, living for herself. I think the culture is paying a price for this.[2]

I read an interview not long ago with John Slattery, one of the actors on "Homefront," another one of the popular new series set in the post-World War II era. He was asked about the source of the success of "Brooklyn Bridge" and some of the other period shows. His answer was simple. "These shows present a different time, when people were less cynical . . . there was less of a looking down your nose at things back then. There was an importance to sitting down together at the dinner table and talking about what happened during the day. In my family, we all had to come home—you had to be there, and that was it."

Barbara Bush said something similar in an interview not long ago. Among the sources of strength in her family growing up were the three daily meals the family took together. Such a seemingly modest ritual is the family rite most at risk when members spend even a slightly extended day on the job or on the commute. This, too, is part of the tradition that all families understand, and that all need to remain vital.

The Generations of Family

The older I get and the more I try to plan for the future, the more I learn that life is full of hairpin turns and last-minute rescues. Today's baby boomers are finding themselves careening toward one of those curves. The biological clock is ticking on the dashboard. Many of the boomers now hear its sound pulsing ever more loudly, ringing in their ears more insistently than the doomsday clocks of Worldwatch or the atomic scientists. Delaying marriage and childbearing, forty-something and over, many boomers are discovering they like keeping house and having children.

The Meaning of Fatherhood

A number of my childless friends have asked me what it is like to be a parent. But I find it impossible to describe to another man how his life will change forever once he becomes a father. There are changes, of course, when one leaves bachelorhood for the joys of matrimony. There is a need to accommodate and compromise with another adult, to engage in the give and take that keeps a marriage together. But these are minor "fine tunings" compared to the major alterations of parenthood. How can I describe to anyone else the emotions you feel when you see a reflection of yourself and your wife in a child's eyes, or walk, or the way a word is pronounced, or the inflection of a voice? How can I capture the sense of total devotion I feel, of being willing to give anything or everything so that this life will flourish? How can I explain the ritual of tiptoeing into a child's bedroom in the evening and in the glow of a night-light looking for reassurance, standing there desperately wanting to see a tiny chest going up and down, or hear a breath, or see a small movement to reaffirm that the divine spark of life is still there. And all the while knowing that if that spark were gone, I would die, too.

You save for them. You work harder for them. You laugh louder with them. You cry deeper over them. You worry unceasingly because of them. And at the end of each exhausting day, you thank God for them. And then you start it all over the next.

When I was growing up I tried to imagine the world without me in it, but I couldn't do it. I was the center of my life. Now I can't imagine joy or love, summer or weekends, Christmas or July 4, sunsets or dawns without *them.* They are the sun around which everything revolves. They are my life.

My friend and author Dale Hanson Bourke has written about the same feelings she has experienced from the perspective of a mother. In her book *Everyday Miracles,* Dale describes having lunch with a girlfriend who is thinking about starting a family. Her friend focuses on the surface changes likely to occur in her life when a baby comes—"no more sleeping in on Saturdays, no more spontaneous vacations." But Dale is thinking about the more profound changes that every mother experiences.

> I want her to know what she will never learn in childbirth classes: that the physical wounds of childbearing heal, but that becoming a mother will leave an emotional wound so raw that she will be forever vulnerable. I consider warning her that she will never read a newspaper again without asking, "What if that had been my child?" That every plane crash, every fire will haunt her. That when she sees pictures of starving children, she will wonder if anything could be worse than watching your child die.
>
> I look at her manicured nails and stylish suit and think that no matter how sophisticated she is, becoming a mother will reduce her to the primitive level of a bear protecting her cub. That an urgent call of Mom! will cause her to drop her best crystal without a moment's hesitation.

> I feel I should warn her that no matter how many years she has invested in her career, she will be professionally derailed by motherhood. She might arrange for child care, but one day she will be going into an important business meeting, and she will think about her baby's sweet smell. She will have to use every ounce of discipline to keep from running home, just to make sure her child is all right. . . .
>
> Looking at my attractive friend, I want to assure her that eventually she will shed the pounds of pregnancy, but she will never feel the same about herself. That her life, now so important, will be of less value to her once she has a child. That she would give it up in a moment to save her offspring, but will also begin to hope for more years—not to accomplish her own dreams, but to watch her child accomplish his.
>
> My friend's relationship with her husband will change, but not in the ways she thinks. I wish she could understand how much more you can love a man who is always careful to powder the baby or who never hesitates to play with his son or daughter. I think she should know that she will fall in love with her husband again for reasons she would now find very unromantic.
>
> I want to describe to my friend the exhilaration of seeing your child learn to hit a baseball. I want to capture for her the belly laugh of a baby who is touching the soft fur of a dog for the first time. I want her to taste the joy that is so real it hurts.

As we race toward the next century, more and more men and women are realizing that this is the path to happiness and meaning in life. As the 1980s unwound, the rate of women in their forties giving birth to a third child had risen 120 percent from the previous decade. For women in their mid- to late-thirties, the increase was 63 percent. For one woman, whose third baby was very much a surprise to herself and her "unflappable executive" husband, the reaction of most of her peers was something of a surprise, too. "Sure, some were shocked," she wrote. "But many more were delighted—even a little envious. A few confessed they were thinking hard about doing the same thing themselves."[3]

In one of his books, C. S. Lewis remarks that when a friend dies, we not only feel the loss directly, but we see that loss reflected in other friends as well. The way the person who is gone used to laugh with this friend or talk to another. We lose that, too. In birth, that is what we gain. Two sisters wrapped up in their own preoccupations, their games and quarrels, suddenly have a little brother on hand, and not only is their relationship with him established, but a new one is made with each other, and with their parents as well. A kindness appears. A maturity develops.

"A haven in a heartless world," is what Christopher Lasch called the family. He is right, and a world with many families thereby becomes less heartless, and holds more havens.

Family will always be with us not merely because it offers us overpowering joys, but, in an odd way, because of its griefs too. Each joy and grief is an aspect of the love to which human beings aspire, both to give and to receive.

I don't listen to a lot of rock music these days, but someone recently showed me an article about guitarist Eric Clapton's ballad, "Tears in Heaven." I remembered seeing the front-page photograph in the *New York Post* of the singer's three-year-old son, Conor, lying dead on a rooftop in New York, where he had eluded the watchful eye of his nanny and fallen from a high window. My own son was just a little older at the time. It tore at me.

My heart still stops every time the news anchor's voice breaks in on the radio, "Police report a four-year-old boy . . ." That lead is almost never good news; it's often the worst.

The heart gained by family is sometimes broken. Maybe it always is. The bravado of youth often says, "I'd give my life to . . ." Becoming a parent is knowing that there are things, people for which you really would give your life.

I think of how, in the midst of wars and treaties, bills signed and contracts inked, ships launched and stock markets crashed, deals struck and promises broken, family still rushes to the fore. How love of family can keep you awake at night and get you up in the morning. How it can get you late to church and early to the poor house.

Parenting

I marvel at the sacrifices and the pains that somehow later come back to seem pleasures in a way, like a hard-fought battle that has been won. They characterize family life. It is what we live for; it is what we work for. It is what we never have enough time for. I think of those long nights when a fevered child is placed into a bathtub full of tepid water. How hard it is to explain that this is for his own good. I think of the falls and accidents and trips to the emergency room that every family with children has experienced.

There are the broken bones and broken hearts, a school election lost, or a gymnastic meet that ended with a fall from the beam. I remember colic and the mysterious illness that laid Sarah so low. She stopped walking. She slept twenty-three hours a day and couldn't find the strength to chew or even drink. I remember putting water into her mouth with a food baster so she wouldn't spit it out, the doctors who couldn't explain to us what was wrong, the exhaustion and the surrender of prayer. Then finally like a miracle after two weeks, she suddenly lifted her head, pushed herself off Carol's lap and walked again. My relief that it was finally over, and my fear that some silent virus could hurt my child so much while we helplessly watched. Zack's night terrors, stolen bikes, schoolyard fights, report cards, baptisms, graduation, honor roll breakfasts, handmade Father's and Mother's Day cards. The mementos jammed into my briefcase, pictures of all of them carried on each business trip in the belief that somehow I can protect them if I can see their image.

Then after all of this, we are left with a paradox. We can't have the satisfaction of a shipbuilder or a craftsman who can rightfully say, "I completed this work; it is mine." We look at our children and say, "I participated in this work, but God, it is yours." After all of the joy and the agony, the victories and the defeats, after sleepless nights and too early mornings, after countless cries and hugs in the night, after discipline and arguments, the process is completed and then the child must walk on its own. And so the next agony awaits, rehearsed dozens of times before, on the first day of kindergarten, or the first date, the agony of seeing them fly from us and find their own way.

Yet they are always our children. I never quite understood in my teenage years, when I was straining to grow up and be my own man, what my mother meant when she told me that I would always be her child. But now I do. A good friend of mine, a businessman in his late fifties, told me how his nineteen-year-old daughter asked him in disgust one day, "Dad, when are you going to stop treating me like a child?" To which he replied, "When my seventy-seven-year-old mother stops treating me like one."

The cycle is eternal. It is scarier and more exhilarating than the steepest amusement park roller coaster. It was done by our parents and theirs before them. It will be done by our children and by theirs. It is the unbelievably challenging, overwhelmingly gratifying way that we were meant to live.

I think of the long history of families, American families, and know in my heart that there is an even longer future. The words of ballads and hymns may change, but the mystic cords of family bind alike. Home is a sacred and mystical place, an image of heaven. "Then would I find a settled rest," the hymn sings,

> While others go and come,
> No more a stranger nor a guest
> But like a child at home.[4]

Have we been through a war over family? We retreated to the family in previous wars. I think of Union soldier Elisha Hunt Rhodes, writing in a letter during a break in the fighting near the Rapidan River in Central Virginia, not far from where my family and I live today. A hard rain was falling. "All night," he wrote, "the battle raged, and we had to lay there. Sleep would overpower us when we were not firing and such dreams as I had. I dreamt that I was home and so warm and comfortable sitting by the fire with mother and sister when some one says our lines are giving way"—and the battle raged anew.

I think of Robert E. Lee, sitting in his tent trying to focus on some official papers of the war. An officer comes upon him as he sits in tears, unable to work because of the "anguish" he cannot put out of his mind at the news of the loss of his twenty-three-year-old daughter, "my sweet Annie."

I think, too, of Abraham Lincoln, leaving Illinois for Washington, destiny and the great crisis before him, bidding his neighbors farewell and speaking of his sorrow at leaving home, "Here the most sacred ties of earth were assumed; here all my children were born, and here one of them lies buried."

I think of Mark Twain, whose humor caused a nation to laugh, but who knew the unparalleled misery of outliving his wife and three of his four children. Of his remorse, losing his only son at twenty-two months, of how he blamed himself for the child's illness, because of a carriage ride on a "raw, cold morning." Twain tearfully wrote later that he had "forgot all about" the child sitting beside him and the furs in which he was wrapped fell away, exposing "his bare legs" and leaving him "almost frozen." That ride haunted him the rest of his life.

In the grief of a parent's love, Twain borrowed from an Australian poet's words and had them inscribed on his daughter Susie's tombstone:

> Warm summer sun shine kindly here;
> Warm southern wind blow softly here;
> Green sod above, lie light, lie light—
> Good night, dear heart, good night, good night.

Then the last, and perhaps the worst for him, on Christmas Eve 1909, his daughter Jean. He visits the rooms where only hours before she had been alive and busy:

> I have been to Jean's parlor. Such a turmoil of Christmas presents for servants and friends! They are everywhere; tables, chairs, sofas, the floor—everything is occupied and over-occupied. It is many and many a year since I have seen the like.

> In that ancient day Mrs. Clemens and I used to slip softly into the nursery at midnight on Christmas Eve and look the array of presents over. The children were little then. And now here is Jean's parlor looking just as that nursery used to look. The presents are not labeled—the hands are forever idle that would have labeled them today.[5]

Remembering

The Vietnam Memorial, born in controversy like the war from which it sprang, is now the most popular site for visitors in Washington, D.C. The black granite slab listing the names of America's sons and daughters who gave "the last full measure of devotion" is the product of a nationwide artistic competition. Many felt the winning design was too bleak and negative, a protest in itself of the war long after it was over. But how could its designer or any of us know beforehand how the monument would be changed each day by the love of the American people and that on no two days would it be exactly the same?

The daily alterations are made by grieving parents, sisters, brothers, former comrades-in-arms, old loves, children who only knew a father's name, friends, and classmates. Each day these people come and leave mementos at the base or in the crevices of the monument which no artist could capture in the finest granite with the surest hand. There they sit, letters never sent, a wedding ring, a school annual, a fresh flower, an old coat perhaps worn by an adolescent front-yard soldier, a lace handkerchief damp with tears, a cross or a charm with no significance to anyone except the person who lovingly placed it there. Each night they are carefully collected by the park rangers. But the next day all new memories are left behind. These things have more power than any of Washington's movers and shakers could ever hope to have. Presidents come and go, but this love of family, this faith in the future, these tears of sacrifice—they are America. They are our hope now and tomorrow.

Our best possessions cost little but are most valuable. The ballads and the verse and the elegiac prose. The love songs, the Mother's Day cards, the flowers "she" loved best. "Our song," the hatbox holding photographs from Coney Island. The wedding bands and family reunions. The baby booties, incredibly small. The baptismal and wedding gowns in the family for generations. The family Bible passed from old hands to young, its tattered cover bearing the names of the ones who went before and who believed. It would take a mighty force to blot out a word of it, much less all of it. Family is too deep. It partakes of the eternal, and we common people know it even when the sophisticates have forgotten.

Faith

In August 1941, with the darkness of world war descending upon us, President Franklin D. Roosevelt met with Prime Minister Winston Churchill aboard a U.S. Navy cruiser off Newfoundland. Churchill had crossed the U-boat-infested Atlantic on a British warship. At the conclusion of their summit, the hard-pressed statesmen led the crews of the two ships in singing "Onward, Christian Soldiers." Because the meeting was secret, there was no one to complain that the heads of government were violating the separation of church and state. Many of the sailors present had already faced the threat of Nazi submarines and Luftwaffe air strikes just to come to the summit. There was a sense of the seriousness of the times and the need for spiritual sustenance. President Roosevelt proclaimed America's commitment to Four Freedoms: Freedom of Speech, Freedom from Fear, Freedom from Want, and Freedom of Worship.

Those four freedoms were soon memorialized by America's beloved illustrator, Norman Rockwell. Visitors to our National Archives can see them today. It is worthwhile to study these popular prints and what they tell us about America then. Rockwell chose to show freedom of speech as a New England town meeting. An earnest workman stands up, proud to address the group, his gnarled hands gripping the church pew in front of him. In his pocket, we see rolled up the town's annual report. His neighbors look at him with expressions of interest and bemusement. Freedom from fear is depicted by two middle-aged parents tucking their small children into bed. Dad holds a newspaper whose headlines decry the terror bombing of civilians in a distant European city. Mom hovers protectively. Rockwell shows freedom from want as a family scene with grandparents preparing to carve a holiday turkey as grateful relatives wait to receive it.

For Norman Rockwell's freedom of worship scene, he offers us a moving scene, a collage of Americans in prayer. It is a culturally and ethnically diverse group. A young, blonde Catholic woman grasps rosary beads. A rabbi in the foreground holds a prayer book, his eyes cast downward in deepest study. An elderly couple pray together, as if from decades of practice. And a black lady, her dignified face bearing the signs of suffering, raises her eyes and hands heavenward in supplication.

This and not the image of intolerance and hostility is the ideal image of American life that we presented to ourselves and to others when we were under a most serious threat. Standing against a monstrous tyranny, a cruel pagan philosophy, we drew together as one people. Norman Rockwell was beloved by Americans because he celebrated the inherent decency and fairness of common people of this land.

Those who have campaigned so intolerantly against the public expression of religious belief, especially in our schools, are warring not only on individuals and communities of belief, but also on an America that was capable of pulling together to defeat Nazi totalitarianism. For it is in freedom of worship that we see the sources of the other three of President Roosevelt's famous Four Freedoms. From a deep attachment to our own religious faith, we can derive the respect for the opinions of others we see in Rockwell's town meeting. From our faith, we gain strength to provide for our material needs and the impetus to share with others, as expressed in freedom from want. Finally, freedom to worship reinforces those values of the home, of security for children, of protection for families that we see so movingly portrayed in freedom from fear.

The truth is, the American people are not embarrassed about their roots in family and religious faith. It would take more than legal changes to uproot those origins; it would take a major face-lift of Washington's monuments. Many writers have pointed out the indelible evidence incised in granite and marble, from the carving of the tablet of the Ten Commandments on the walls of the Justices' chamber at the Supreme Court to the quotations from Jefferson on the slabs of the memorial that bears his name.

But it is a living tradition, too, as a recent trip to the National Air and Space Museum reminded me. The most-visited museum in Washington (maybe that says something about our national character, too—it is largely a trophy collection, a monument to individual and national achievement), Air and Space holds a vast array of artifacts of America's role in air travel and space flight. It also has an IMAX theater, a curved, five-story screen for the projection of the breathtakingly wide IMAX images. The technology has spread to museums around the country, taking with it the IMAX films, including *The Dream Is Alive,* a tribute to the men and women of our space shuttle program.

One of the most recent additions to the IMAX repertoire is a film called *Antarctica.* When my family and I went to see it, we were prepared to see some rare and spectacular scenery and for the comically surreal footage of penguins striding and sliding across the ice. But we were not prepared for the film's powerfully moving finale—not the least because of my slim knowledge of the continent and its brief history of exploration.

The film closes with realistically dramatized scenes of the tragic final days of the Scott Expedition to the South Pole. Robert Scott's five-man team was in competition with a separate team led by the famed explorer Roald Amundsen. The Scott party made the long, bitter trek to the Pole, only to find that Amundsen had reached there four weeks earlier. The return trip was worse. One man died early on. Another was lamed by frostbite and deliberately sacrificed himself, separating from the group to avoid slowing them down and dooming them all.

The other three, including Scott, struggled on, until overtaken by a blizzard just eleven miles from their base camp and safety. One of them, Wilson, wrote these last words to his mother in his journal as the cold and the inevitability of death sank into the men:

> I should so like to have come through for your dear sake. It is splendid to pass however with such companions as I have. And as all five of us have mothers and wives, you will not be alone. Your ever loving son, to the end of this life and the next, when God shall wipe away all tears from our eyes.

The scene then cuts to the present, where the real, live successors of Scott and Amundsen are gathered around the dinner table at an Antarctic research station. One of the men leads the company in a prayer of thanksgiving that concludes, "We just thank you Father for the food that was prepared for us, and we just pray that you will keep us safe and protect us as we work down here. For it's in your name we pray, Amen."

Across boundaries of space and time, separated from home and loved ones, living or dying in the most hostile environment on the planet, these scientists and explorers partake of traditions that have always been part of our national character. And that character, like the dream of space exploration, is indeed alive.

We Are Americans

We have all felt the same despair when we see the headlines about child abuse, rape, violence, drugs, racism, and poverty. Something, we sense, at the very core is going wrong in America.

With so many problems facing us, it is no wonder that the national mood is dark. What may be surprising, however, is that in spite of all of these seemingly intractable problems, most

Americans still believe in the same solid values that animated their parents' and their grandparents' lives. Millions of Americans from all races and economic backgrounds have resisted the cultural pressures and built strong, stable families. Many more are doing their best to make the bone stronger where it has been broken, to set the sights of their children on a better and loftier height.

Americans are ready for a rebirth of the values and commitments that have served us so well in the past and that hold out the only hope for a future that works. The value of sticking to a task even when the reward is months or even years away. The value of honoring the older generation. Of demonstrating strength by protecting the weak in our midst. Of paying more attention to the daily heroes in your own house or the house next door.

With all our problems, almost none of us is lining up at the door to leave America. Instead, this nation of immigrants opens its international mail every day to find a waiting list of people from every corner of the globe who want to join us here. We have no walls to keep people in. We even hesitate to build them to keep people out. Other nations may have museums honoring the pathways of immigrants to their shores, but none that I know of makes a place like Ellis Island a focal point of its civic pride.

Former Education Secretary Bill Bennett, whom I served under, used to talk about what he called the "gates test": Confronted by a student who could perceive no moral difference between a totalitarian Soviet Union and a free United States, Bennett asked the student to consider what happens "at the gates." In the Soviet Union, the gates were closed, yet people risked their lives to get out. In America the gates are open, but the flow of humanity is always toward us. People risk their lives to get in.

There is something about this land that makes nearly all of us think we were here at the beginning. That we rode in on some *Mayflower* of the mind. Yes, that pride can breed misunderstanding and discord. So many of our ancestors arrived jammed on a freighter's deck or chained below it. But it is not the particulars of our history but the ideas of our destiny that bind us together. What Lincoln meant when he spoke of us as "an almost chosen people."

In the end, it is really not our way to think of ourselves as "boats against the tide," as people "borne back ceaselessly into the past." For out of our imperfect pasts, we Americans still see the perfect as being somehow within our scope. We see America still greening, still young, still a nation of families.

Faith about Family

We have a gross national product. An index of leading economic indicators. Standard & Poor's and the Dow-Jones. Nielsen and Arbitron. What we do not have is a single index of the most important indicator of the health of our society: the well-being of families.

Moreover, misplaced emphasis on any one of these other indicators can give us a misreading about family, and thus a misreading of our society. Growing economic output is generally a boon to society. But we must be wary when it is being paid for with the consumption of human capital. A climb in labor force participation may be a sign of boom times. But it may also mean that families are being forced to send both mother and father into the marketplace just to stay afloat, to pay a crushing tax burden, or to hold on to some portion of what they've gained.

I am as concerned as anyone about our nation's ability to remain competitive and our citizens' ability to produce a high standard of living. When I was at the Department of Education, and now here in these pages, I helped to set forth time and again some distressing news about the achievement levels of American students, and surely, as worrisome as some of the absolute numbers were, it was the international comparisons that wrinkled my brow most. We fear falling behind the Japanese one day, the Germans the next.

But for all I read about America's growing competitive disadvantage, I know few people, leaders or ordinary citizens, who would trade our way of life for any other. That goes for our family life, too. Yes, virtually every family in Japan is intact. Only Sweden outstrips us in out-of-wedlock births. Divorce laws are more family-destructive here than in all but a handful of Western countries.

It is just that—and we know this in our hearts—our blessings transcend our difficulties, our resources exceed our problems, our character outmatches our flaws. Time is the great healer, and history is the great consoler. Much of what we perceive as America's economic glory years came about under conditions no sane person would want to repeat. We bested the major industrialized nations for a generation because so many of them had been devastated by war. We stood in the breach to defend our allies and paid the price in blood and toil, but the destruction rained on their cities and factories, not on ours.

When V-E Day came, we turned our full attention to the aggressors in the Pacific. And when the peace was purchased with massive firepower and loss of life, we stepped in to assure that Imperial Japan would not rise from the ashes to rearm itself and threaten us ever again. Like a boxer who knows he has the bout in hand, we helped these staggered nations to their feet. Our competitive edge was in large part a temporary condition, the only fruit of war we claimed, and not one we sought for ourselves.

Now that the field has shifted somewhat, and the war-ravaged economies of the Far East and Europe are robust (at least wherever freedom lives), we have more to celebrate than to regret. A healthy concern for America's future growth, its ability to innovate and achieve, makes sense. A mad dash for competitive advantage, at the expense of family values, makes no sense at all. If having a loving mother and father in the home matters more to educational success, for example, than either the length of the school year or per capita education spending, we would be mad to violate family time or raise family taxes through the roof for a crash program of education "reform."

Our schools can do remarkably better than they are. They should certainly be absolutely safe. But it may well be that our nation's commitment to educate everyone—and our nation's hospitality to other cultures and to people from every part of the world—will forever mean that we seem a shade behind more homogeneous societies.

We must be homogeneous, mind you. One in our commitment to family, faith, and freedom. Unified in our determination to keep this republic the Framers built. Focused on our task of teaching the next generation the idea and the ideal that America represents. We must rededicate ourselves to excellence, but we must always remember that excellence is a personal virtue before it is ever a civic value.

It would be a dark day for America if we awoke one morning to find our factories humming and our towers of glass and stainless steel teeming with busy executives, but with no trace of family. With no one gathered around dinner tables to talk about the day's events, with no time for anyone to volunteer at the nursing home or the Y, with no private economy where a cup of sugar is traded for an hour of baby-sitting, with back fences too high for talking, with no Major League Baseball games played anywhere on Wednesday afternoons.

The hurried urban pace of the 1950s gave us the term "rat race." Maybe that's where part of our troubles began. America does need a resurgence of the work ethic, yes. A renewal of pride and excellence. But we must begin by working anew at our family life. Being a good father, a sacrificing mother, a dedicated son, a loyal daughter. These are the cornerstones on which a nation's economic house is built.

Crossroads

How will history ultimately judge us? Will it remember those hardy pioneers, families in tow, who tamed the wilderness? Or will America's legacy be decaying cities and crime-ridden streets? Our last chapter hasn't been written yet. There is still time to reach down into the deep reservoir of hearth and home. We can put family at the center of our lives again and rededicate ourselves to our children and to each other. We can rebuild strong neighborhoods and stop sinking further into the quagmire that recognizes nothing as right or wrong, true or false. We can recognize that our greatest wealth is not in steel and iron, gold and oil, but in the love that binds us together and the heritage given us by strong men and women who believed in something. We can teach our children the difference between love and sex, remind each other of the reasons for fidelity and faithfulness. We can rediscover the God who first dedicated our nation and to whom we appeal as the author of our liberty.

Or we can continue down the road many have traveled in recent years. We can so redefine what a family is that the word will no longer have meaning. We can continue putting everything else before our children—our jobs, our hobbies, our possessions, our temptations—until we lose most of them to a culture that offers sex, drugs, and living for today. We can break all the taboos, ignore our heritage, forget those who went before, ignore those yet to come, spend the capital built up over the ages and never add anything to replenish it. We can give each child a personal supply of pills and condoms, make sure our addicts have clean needles, abort our unwanted children, ignore our wedding vows, indulge for today, and forget about tomorrow.

What we cannot do is both. As we go forward in this last decade of the twentieth century, we can't continue with two diametrically opposed value systems. Ultimately our public philosophy will embrace family, faith, and freedom, or it will embrace pleasure now. Either we will reteach character or we will pretend values don't matter. The "genie" of sexual irresponsibility will either be put back into the bottle of self-restraint or we will cave in to the marketplace offering flesh but no commitment.

A society cannot ultimately survive with two such starkly opposed philosophies. Strong families can't be islands surrounded by an "anything goes" culture. You can't teach some children that some things are right and some wrong while you slip condoms to other children under the table. You can't extend all the rights and privileges of marriage to live-in lovers and homosexual couples and expect the heterosexual family to thrive. You can't rediscover our religious heritage and censure children who pray.

I began by saying I am an optimist, and I am. At long last the battle is being joined. We are ready for a national debate on the kind of people we are and where we want to go. Much of this battle will be in the political and legislative arena. But the most important part will be in our hearts and our own homes. We must begin now to rebuild our nation, one house at a time.

> How small, of all that human hearts endure,
> That part which laws or kings can cause or cure.
>
> Samuel Johnson

Endnotes

Chapter 1 • Going Home

1. Douglas Southall Freeman, *George Washington* (New York: Charles Scribner's Sons, 1952), 5:477–78.
2. Carl Sandburg, *Abraham Lincoln, The War Years* (New York: Charles Scribner's Sons, 1948), 412.
3. Suzanne Chazin, "Long Journey Home," *Reader's Digest* (November 1991): 83–86.
4. "Open Arms for the Queen," *Washington Post,* 26 May 1991.

Chapter 2 • Our Dreams

1. Stuart Elliott, "KFC's Very Real Problems May Be Solved in Lake Edna," *New York Times,* 19 May 1992.
2. Joe Klein, "Whose Values?" *Newsweek,* 8 June 1992, 22.
3. Josh McDowell and Dick Day, *Why Wait? What You Need to Know about the Teen Sexuality Crisis* (San Bernardino, Calif.: Here's Life Publishers, 1987), 15.
4. Lawrence M. Mead, "The New Politics of the New Poverty," *The Public Interest,* no. 103 (Spring 1991): 10.
5. "Va. Mother and 2 Sons Perish in Fire," *Washington Post,* 9 April 1992, C-1.
6. "MassMutual American Family Values Study: Results of Focus Group and Survey Research," research conducted by Mellman & Lazarus, Washington, D.C., undated report obtained from MassMutual Life Insurance Co., p. 15.
7. Zig Ziglar, *Possibilities Magazine* (March–April 1990).
8. Deborah L. Cohen, "Restoring Nation's Moral Order Starts with Families," *Education Week,* 27 November 1991.

Chapter 3 • The Good News

1. Archibald Rutledge, *Peace in the Heart* (New York: Doubleday, 1927), cited in *Reader's Digest* (May 1992): 155.
2. "The Simple Life," *Time,* 8 April 1991, 62–63.
3. "Whose Values?" *Newsweek,* 8 June 1992, 20.
4. Karl Zinsmeister, "Raising Children in a Difficult Age," in *Who Will Rock the Cradle?* ed. Phyllis Schlafly (Dallas: Word, 1990), 27.
5. Brad Edmondson, "Burned-Out Boomers Flee to Families," *American Demographics* (December 1991): 17.
6. "Trouble at the Top," *U.S. News & World Report,* 17 June 1991, 42.
7. Terri L. Darrow, "The Sequencing of Motherhood," *Kiwanis Magazine* (March 1992): 35.
8. "Proceeding with Caution," *Time,* 16 July 1990, 58.
9. Michael Kaplan, "You Can Go Home Again," *Ad Week,* 7 May 1990, 14–15.
10. "Family Time Is More Important than Rapid Career Advancement," *Supervision* (March 1990): 13.
11. Carol Hymowitz, "Trading Fat Paychecks for Free Time," *Wall Street Journal,* 5 August 1991, B1.
12. Stephen Schaefer, "Weaver, Performing Strong," *USA Today,* 20 May 1992, D1.
13. Tom Green, "Patriot Star Settles Far from L.A.," *USA Today,* 5 June 1992, D1–2.
14. "Things They Said," *World Magazine,* 23 May 1992, 4.
15. Sarah Ban Breathnach, "Living in a Lower Gear," *Washington Post,* 31 December 1991, C5.
16. "Prognosticator Plugs into Teens' Thoughts, Dreams," *USA Today,* 22 January 1992, D3.
17. "America's Holy War," *Time,* 9 December 1991, 68.

Chapter 4 • More Good News

1. "Get Me to the Church on Time," Associated Press, 27 April 1992.
2. Sonya Friedman, "Murphy Brown's Distorted Picture Ignores Reality of Single Mothering," *Detroit Free Press,* 20 May 1992.
3. Barbara Dafoe Whitehead, "What Is Murphy Brown Saying?" *Washington Post,* 10 May 1992.
4. George Will, "God Don't Make Junk," *Washington Post,* 29 March 1992, C7.
5. Michael Medved, "Has Hollywood Gone Too Far?" *USA Weekend,* 27–29 March 1992, 4.
6. Richard Zoglin, "Upscale and Uplifting," *Time,* 27 April 1992, 64–65.

7. L. Douglas Wilder, "To Save the Black Family, the Young Must Abstain," *Wall Street Journal,* 28 March 1991.
8. National Commission on Children, *Beyond Rhetoric: A New American Agenda for Children and Families* (Washington, D.C.: Government Printing Office, 1991), 344.
9. Emory University-Grady Memorial Hospital Family Planning Program, *The Joy of Birth Control* (U.S. Department of Health, Education and Welfare Grant #04-H-000311-04-0, Georgia Department of Human Resources, contract #900398) undated booklet, circa 1974, 2d ed. 1977. The Department of Health, Education and Welfare (HEW) was the predecessor to the U.S. Department of Health and Human Services (HHS).
10. National Commission on Children, *Beyond Rhetoric,* 224–25.
11. Judy Mann, "What's So Bad about Abstinence?" *Washington Post,* 24 April 1992, E3.
12. Jana Mazanec, "Birthrate Soars at Colo[rado] School," *USA Today,* 19 May 1992, A3.

Chapter 5 • What Every Parent Must Do

1. Patrick M. Morley, *The Man in the Mirror* (Brentwood, Tenn.: Wolgemuth & Hyatt, 1989), 89.
2. Bob V. Mouler, "Sounds of Home," condensed from *Ford Times, Reader's Digest* (June 1988): 143–44.
3. National Commission on Children, *Beyond Rhetoric: A New American Agenda for Children and Families* (Washington, D.C.: Government Printing Office, 1991), 211.
4. James S. Coleman, "Parental Involvement in Education," in *Policy Perspectives* (June 1991), a series published by the Office of Educational Research and Improvement, U.S. Department of Education.
5. Charles Neider, ed., *The Autobiography of Mark Twain* (New York: Harper & Row, 1959), 30.
6. Coleman, "Parental Involvement in Education," 13.
7. "Homeward Bound," *Focus on the Family* (January 1992): 7.

Chapter 6 • What Every Child Should Be Taught

1. James A. Michener, "What Is the Secret of Teaching Values?" *Fortune,* 25 March 1991, 78–79.
2. Henry Hyde, *For Every Idle Silence* (Ann Arbor, Mich.: Servant, 1985), 107.
3. NBC News Special, "City Under Fire," 1 May 1992.
4. S. Robert Chiappinelli, "Gossett: Family Is Antidote to Violence," *Providence Journal-Bulletin,* 4 May 1992, A1.

Chapter 7 • The Literature of Family, Faith, and Freedom

1. Barbara Bush, "Parenting's Best Kept Secret: Reading to Your Children," *Reader's Digest* (October 1990): 67–70.
2. C. S. Lewis, *The Lion, the Witch and the Wardrobe* (New York: Collier Books, 1970).
3. David McCullough, *Brave Companions* (New York: Prentice-Hall, 1992), 223.

Chapter 8 • Rediscovering America

1. Tom Shales, "Brooklyn, a Wistful Trip Home," *Washington Post,* 20 September 1991.
2. "Marion Ross, Peerless Mainstay of Brooklyn Bridge," *Washington Post,* TV Week, 7–13 June 1992, 6–7.
3. Eileen Ogintz, "And Baby Makes . . . Five," *Boston Globe Sunday Magazine,* 26 April 1991, 19.
4. Isaac Watts, "My Shepherd Will Supply My Need."
5. Charles Neider, ed., *The Autobiography of Mark Twain* (New York: Harper & Row, 1959), 373–74.